D1561795

Treating Attachment Abuse

Steven Stosny, PhD, Director of the Community Outreach Service, which serves clients in and around Washington, DC, received his doctorate in clinical social work from the University of Maryland at Baltimore. He has treated more than 600 perpetrators and victims of various forms of attachment abuse and is the author of books, articles, and chapters about various forms of abuse. During the past 5 years Dr. Stosny has developed the Compassion Workshop, and has worked with a highly varied population of abusers and victims. His passion about attachment abuse grew from his childhood experience in a violent home.

Treating Attachment Abuse

A Compassionate Approach

Steven Stosny, PhD

Springer Publishing Company

Springer Publishing Company, Inc.
536 Broadway
New York, NY 10012-3955

Cover design by Tom Yabut
Production Editor: Pam Lankas

95 96 97 98 99 / 5 4 3 2 1

Library of Congress Cataloging-in-Publication Data

Stosny, Steven.
Treating attachment abuse : a compassionate approach / Steven Stosny.
p. cm.
Includes bibliographical reference and index.
ISBN 0-8261-8960-1
1. Psychological abuse. 2. Attachment behavior. 3. Caring. I. Title.
RC569.5.P75S76 1995
616.85′82—dc20 95-7295
CIP

Printed in the United States of America

To my mother,
from whose suffering
this treatment was born

Contents

Introduction

The treatment described in these pages offers a systematic approach to an often underestimated reason that people seek the help of clinicians. Nearly everyone who goes into counseling, for whatever reason, does so in the throes of failed *self-compassion.* Such failure, prominent in symptom-formation, eventually depletes compassion for others, as it disables natural self-healing and self-nurturing capacities, in effect, suppressing the immune system of the psyche and rendering self-regulation arduous and painful.

COMPASSION AND SELF-BUILDING

As the salient attachment emotion, compassion plays a key role in the *self-building* function of the innate attachment drive. "Self-building" refers to the unique power of interactions among attachment figures to build an individual's sense of self, particularly personal value as an attachment figure: whether one is worthy of love and whether one's love is worthy of others. Obviously, the stakes of self-building loom high, with emotional rewards among the greatest of human experience: love and secure attachment. These, in turn, stimulate deeper self-compassion, in a kind of happy feedback loop, depicted in Figure I.1.

Figure I.1
Compassion and self-building.

Compassion for self ⟶	**Compassion for others** ⟶	**Emotional inter-** ⟶ **regulation**	**Self-building** ⟶	**Interest Trust Love Security**
understanding internal experience	understanding experience of others		development of the loving and loveable self	
valadating internal experience	validating experience of others			
changing validated internal experience (negative meanings about the self)	supporting or empowering others to change validated internal experience (negative meanings about the self)			

FAILED COMPASSION AND ABUSE

Failures of compassion transform the self-building function of attachment relationships into a potentially self-destroying process. By virtue of the emotional inter-regulation that sustains emotional bonds (and in which compassion plays so crucial a role), attachment figures serve as nothing less than mirrors of the inner self. *Attachment abusers* are those who fall prey to the illusion that they can blame attachment figures for the intolerable shame of feeling unlovable or inadequate as loving agents, that is, they blame the mirror for the reflection. To the extent that they try to manipulate, coerce, or force change in the mirror to modulate or transform internal experience, they abuse their loved ones, while, ironically,

Figure I.2 Failure to compassion: Abuse of self and/or others.

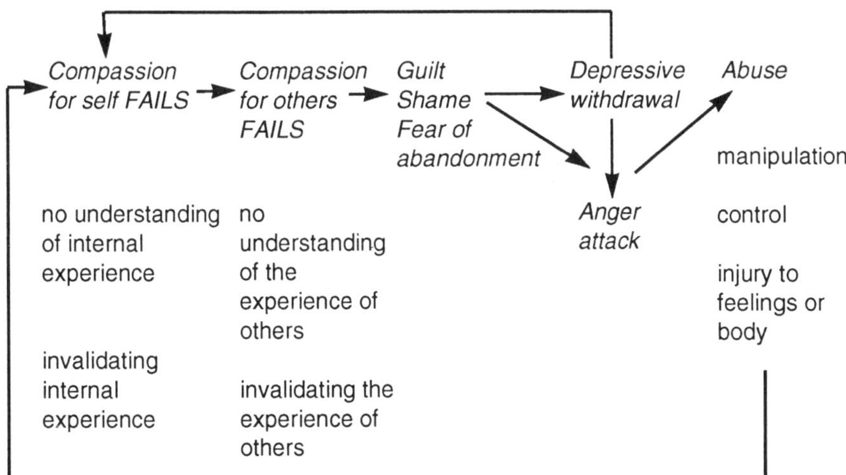

remaining entirely powerless over their own thoughts, feelings, and action impulse (that which, uninhibited and unconstrained, becomes overt behavior). Once again, the personal stakes are high, as self-building failures carry the heaviest of emotional penalties: rejection, shame, and abandonment-terror, which stimulate alternating states of anger and depression, as depicted in the negative feedback loop of Figure I.2.

THE COMPASSION WORKSHOP

The Compassion Workshop consists of a series of treatment modules designed to relieve the self-building deficits of both perpetrators and victims of attachment abuse. The discreet modules of the Workshop can serve as adjuncts to individual, group, or family therapy where abuse is a risk. In combination, the six modules have been adapted for structured group treatment of more serious (i.e., violent and overtly psychologically damaging) child, intimate partner, and elder abusers. In and around the nation's capital, the treatment, applied individually, in families, and in groups, has proven effective at 1-year follow-ups at all socioeconomic levels, from the chronically unemployed to high officials in government, professional athletes, attorneys, and construction workers. We have even successfully run groups that mixed violent child and elder abusers of both genders with heterosexual, lesbian, and gay partner abusers.

The unusual flexibility of the treatment owes to its focus on the fundamental, survival-based human drive to attach, which entails susceptibility to a continuum of abusive behaviors (See Figure I.3). These range from insensitively hurting the feelings of a loved one (through inadvertent failure of compassion) to life-threatening violence. The temporary self-enhancing arousal (anger, excitation, or intensified focus) characteristic of abuse varies in degree of intensity from one abusive act to another along the continuum.

Most of us most of the time manage to stop at the first two or three rungs on the abuse continuum. We avoid the moderate and extreme forms of abuse, not through control of anger and hostility, or through threats of legal sanctions, or even through the threat of guilt, shame, and abandonment-terror, but through activation of our innate capacity for compassion. In other words, we avoid abuse, not to escape punishment, but for the internal reward of compassion: its ability to build the powerful sense of self that ultimately renders the privilege of moral agency. It will be argued in these pages that compassion, as the salient form of intimate emotional inter-regulation necessary to establish attachment bonds, activates the psychobiological substrata of moral agency. That same moral agency requires that we help those who have eroded their self-esteem and brutalized the compassionate part of themselves, doing ultimate destruction to themselves in hurting those they love.

Because the occasional failure of compassion (that leads us to deliberately or inadvertently hurt the feelings of loved ones) occurs universally in intimate relationships, enhancement of attachment bonds through training in compassion

Figure I.3 Failures of Compassion.

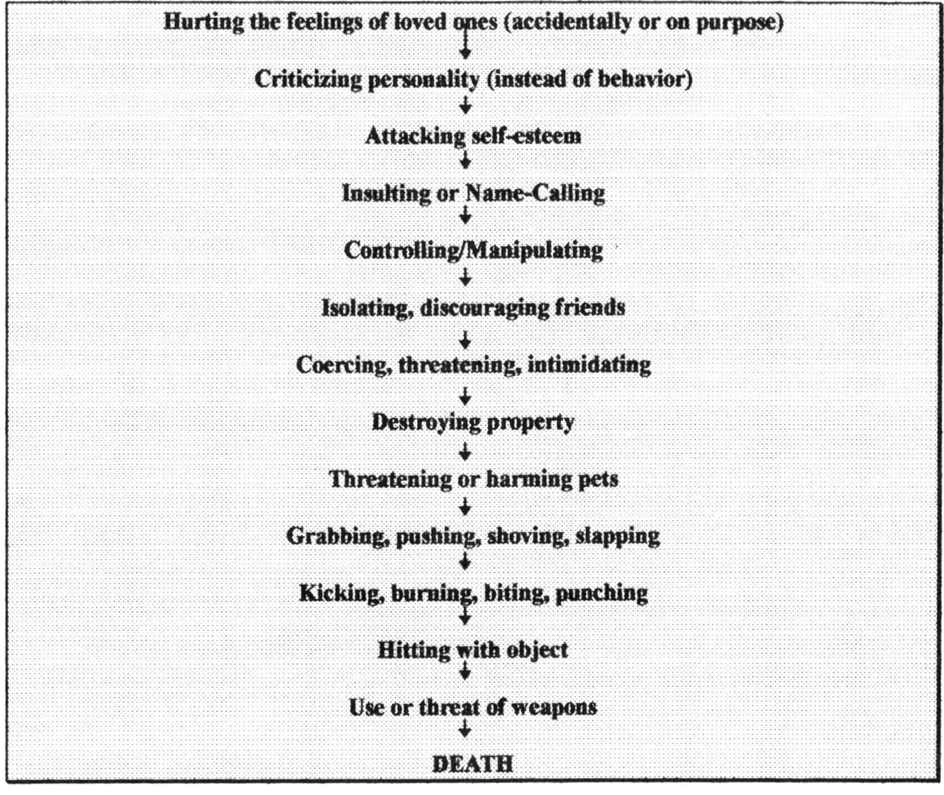

serves as a common goal to be pursued without the formidable resistance endemic to conventional treatment for abusers. Due to its strategic place as the first leg on the continuum of abuse, the elimination of failures of compassion prevents progression along the track of pain that ends too often in violence and death.

It must be emphasized that the current volume constitutes a clinical or micro-level analysis of a phenomenon that, in its most extreme forms, has become a public health problem with potent macro-level influences. (Indeed, many authors have discussed these influences eloquently in reference to a culture of violence and social injustice.) It behooves us to acknowledge that all micro interventions are embedded in social and cultural contexts. Questions of individual differences, however—why some people in common social and cultural contexts damage their children, elder parents, and lovers while many do not—lead clinicians to consider the innate mechanisms of attachment, which play a necessary role in the formation of intimate relationships and social bonds. This book is for those clinicians who treat individuals, families, and groups of people who have difficulties with attachment and social bonds. It claims a breadth that ranges from social withdrawal to extreme violence against loved ones, only because each of these acts of social and moral disparity begins with a failure of self-compassion.

Part I

The Role of Attachment in Abuse

1 Beginnings: Self-Building, Abuse, and Treatment

Attachment relationships build the selves of children by creating the earliest and deepest meaning they experience. The well-being of the continuously developing self remains so intertwined with the well-being of attachment figures that attachment relationships constitute the primary self-building force throughout life.

To the well-integrated sense of self, attachment relationships contribute:

- the creation and continual confirmation of self-knowledge, especially of one's status as a loving and lovable person;
- validation of the sense of self;
- enhancement and growth of the self;
- the capacity for self-acceptance;
- emotional attunement and inter-regulation, which brings happiness and contentment in domestic life.

In the long run we may live *in* our work, but we live *for* the well-integrated sense of self provided by healthy attachment relationships.

ATTACHMENT ABUSE: CRIMES AGAINST THE SELF

The primary builder of an individual's sense of self, attachment relationships can also serve as the principal self-destroyer, for abuse from no other source can reach so deeply into the structure of self. The very qualities we cherish in attachment relationships create an unparalleled emotional vulnerability to attachment figures.

- The creation and confirmation of self-knowledge (especially one's status as a loving and lovable person) are most distorted and corrupted by attachment figures.
- The emotional attunement and inter-regulation that brings happiness and contentment can be most manipulated, undermined, and exploited by attachment figures.
- Enhancement of the self can be uniquely perverted and obstructed by parents, lovers, and children.
- Self-development can be uniquely and powerfully subverted by attachment figures.
- Self-acceptance can be most encumbered by loved ones.
- An attachment figure's rejection of beliefs and feelings about the self will invalidate one's sense of self.

In summary, the unique self-building (and potentially self-destroying) capacity of the attachment bond forms the heart of all intimate relationship functions and dysfunctions. That which impairs, subverts, distorts, or damages the self-building nature of attachment interaction is rightly regarded as *attachment abuse.*

THE COMPASSION WORKSHOP FOR ATTACHMENT ABUSERS

The self-building capacity of the attachment bond is its most important psychological function and, when abused, the most potent instrument of psychological harm. Therefore, remedial self-building techniques must be an emphasis of effective and lasting treatment for both the causes and effects of attachment abuse. Indeed, all therapists practicing in this era of attachment abuse should have at their disposal a *technology of self-building.* The treatment modules of the Compassion Workshop aim at developing this technology. The six modules can be used collectively, as a single unit of treatment. Alternatively, most of the more than 100 client handouts can be selected and integrated within other treatment modalities.

On the intrapsychic level, the overriding treatment question becomes: What does the abusive experience *mean* to abusers. Here the popular distinction between expressive and instrumental abuse loses significance, for abusers do something more central to their perceived emotional survival than merely employ tactics in social interactions. Fundamentally, they *relieve the self-doubt, feelings of powerlessness, and the weakened or diminished sense of self produced by dysfunctions in self-building, the result of impaired capacity to form viable attachment bonds.*

When experiencing a diminished or weakened sense of self, human beings tend to fill the resulting internal regulatory power-void through *external* regulation of experience, usually through addictions, compulsions, or arousal-driven manipulation and abuse of others. In other words, the rush of arousal fills in gaps in the sense of self, providing a temporary illusion of wholeness and personal power. To numb pain, quell anxiety, and momentarily enhance the damaged sense of self, abusers use the analgesic and stimulant effects of emotional arousal (see Chapter Four). Anger, through its necessary attribution of blame, serves to externalize the guilt, shame, and abandonment anxiety caused by the inability to maintain viable attachment relationships. But once made external, converted vulnerable feelings seem to require external validation. To that end, the abuser's motivation takes on a kind of moral imperative, almost a self-righteousness, in punishing those perceived as persecutors. In the retributive exertion of power over loved ones, abusers achieve an artificial certainty and temporary feeling of power. For this fleeting taste of external power, they render themselves utterly powerless over their actual internal experience and increasingly alienated from their deeper feelings.

For abusers, attitudes and social role expectancies function not as causes of abusive behavior, but as excuses and rationalizations for their cruel choice of pain-relief and self-enhancement. It seemed to us in developing the Compassion Workshop that a relatively brief, intensive treatment was possible if it ignored these superficial but well-defended excuses and rationalizations, *while* providing viable pain-relievers and self-enhancements that render use of destructive ones *unnecessary.* Denial and minimizing need not be confronted directly if the reasons for them were removed, at which point they would be given up voluntarily and readily. To this end, the incremental development of the Compassion Workshop took more than 4 years, and included more than 600 attachment abusers, most of them violent spouse and child abusers.

INHIBITION VERSUS REGULATION

The internal mechanism to relieve discomfort and momentarily enhance the sense of self powers all forms of attachment abuse, from mildly hurting feelings to the murder of a loved one. The severity of acts within these extremes on the abuse continuum is determined by four factors:

1. intensity of the need for pain relief and self-enhancement;
2. inability to achieve nonabusive pain relief and self-enhancement;
3. internal inhibitions to certain kinds of abusive behavior;
4. external constraints on certain kinds of abusive behavior.

Thanks to the heroic efforts and leadership of the child-advocacy and feminist movements, the law is finally beginning to provide the fourth factor in the areas of child and woman abuse. Traditional treatments have focused on number 3 and, to a lesser extent, number 2.

The Compassion Workshop focuses on numbers 1 and 2. The effort is not to inhibit, manage, or control abusive behavior. Rather, the treatment develops the skill to *regulate* dysphoria and the abusive action impulse, that is, convert the destructive action impulse into a self-building experience through the invocation of compassion. This, in turn, provides the moral authority necessary for genuine self-esteem and choice of compassionate behavior.

The Compassion Workshop builds skill in:

1. the use of compassion for self and loved ones as an incompatible response strategy for the internal regulation of negative affect;
2. self-empowerment through lateral (as opposed to hierarchical) self-esteem;
3. empowerment of loved ones;
4. systematic enhancement of the attachment bond, motivated by the therapeutically enhanced internal reward of compassion;
5. negotiating attachment relationships through internal regulation of abandonment and engulfment anxiety.

COMPASSION: INCOMPATIBLE WITH ATTACHMENT ABUSE

In this therapeutic approach, compassion serves, not as a goal, but as the *means* of treatment. The salient emotional motivation to establish and maintain attachment relationships, compassion entails *seeing beneath defenses and symptoms* (anger, anxiety, obsessions, emotional withdrawal, and manipulation), *validating the hurt* causing the symptoms and defenses, and *changing the meaning* that causes the hurt. Thus compassion is a cognitive, emotional, and behavioral experience.

Compassion for self has four dimensions:

1. understanding one's deeper cognitive, affective, and behavioral experience;
2. validation of that experience;
3. motivation to enhance the positive experience and change the meaning of the negative; and

4. self-enhancement through the experience of (1.) through (3.).

Compassion for loved ones has these four dimensions:

1. understanding the attachment figure's cognitive, affective, and behavioral experience (perspective taking);
2. validation of or sympathy with the emotional experience of the attachment figure;
3. motivation to support or enhance the attachment figure; and
4. self-enhancement through the experience of (1.) through (3.).

DEFICITS IN THE NATURAL PREVENTION OF ATTACHMENT ABUSE

Attachment abusers suffer guilt and shame after abuse, but rarely experience the rewards of compassion that prevent abuse. Rather than serve as a deterrent from further abuse, continual guilt and shame tend to lock focus on the self, precluding prosocial motivations and emotions such as compassion (Gilbert, 1992, 1994; Tangney, 1991; Tangney, Wagner, Fletcher, & Gramzow, 1992). This encapsulates abusers in a kind of narcissistic shell in which their own experience, dominated by powerful affect and a variety of coping mechanisms, is merely reflected back at them. Thus insulated from accurate processing of social cues and unmediated by prosocial inhibitions, the temporarily enhancing emotional arousal grows stronger as internal controls, under the painful assault of shame, weaken, permitting full objectification of the victim as nothing more than a source of affect. Research in other behavior problem areas has demonstrated that dysphoria (unrelieved by compassion) creates a high risk of recidivism (Litman, Eiser, Rawson, & Oppenheim, 1975; Marlatt & Gordon, 1985; Neidigh, Gesten, & Shiffman, 1988; Neidigh & Tomiko, 1991). Empirical investigation of these variables with attachment abusers will almost certainly produce similar findings.

Successful treatment of attachment abusers must eliminate the desire for external regulation of experience by providing self-regulatory skill. To the treatment-enhanced Powerful Self, the temporary self-enhancement or analgesia provided by abuse, addictions, or compulsions loom unnecessary. In fact, the mere possibility of addictions, compulsions, and abuse of others takes on immediately aversive qualities, rather than temporarily self-enhancing, titillating, or pleasurable effects. Therapeutic empowerment of the self prevents recidivism of abuse by creating moral agency through enhanced sensitivity to the inner experience of self, which enhances sensitivity to the experience of other people. As it regulates powerful affect, self-compassion lowers the narcissistic shell that precludes compassion for others. It provides that which the self-building deficits of abusers has deprived them: genuine, reality-revealing compassion, to serve as the mortar of their attachment relationships.

COMPASSION CONTRASTED TO PITY AND EMPATHY

The term, "compassion," as used in the Compassion Workshop, implies equality: "I sympathize with your hurt because, despite differences in luck, we're (humanely) equal." "Pity" implies inequality: "I pity you because you're deficient in some way (naive, stupid, uneducated, ugly, poor, unskilled, etc.)."

Compassion provides motivation to understand the experience of another. Projecting one's feelings on another, or putting one's self in the place of another are forms of veiled narcissism incompatible with compassion. Genuine compassion entails understanding and appreciating the *differences* between the self and attachment figures.

Pity can be construed as merely feeling bad at the sight of another's suffering. When this dysphoric feeling is not mediated by sympathy, it can easily lead to contempt. The German playwright, Bertolt Brecht, mused that the first time we see a beggar on the street we'll feel pity for him. The second time, we'll call a policeman to have him removed. This association of contempt with pity comes in part from powerlessness over the unpleasant feelings stimulated by the pitiable. They make us feel guilty for having more, angry at them for not getting better, and frustrated over our inability to make them better.

Similarly, the pain of self-pity breeds self-contempt. "Its so hard being me, having to live in my wretched skin."

In contrast, self-compassion heals as it restores the capacity to repair any real or perceived damage to the self. Compassion for others empowers the self through the experience of understanding, sympathy, and support, without assuming unrealistic responsibility for the results of these gifts on the recipient of compassion. Indeed, such an assumption of responsibility for the internal experience of another (unless a young child) is yet another form of veiled narcissism incompatible with genuine compassion.

The greatest inhibitor of pity is the fear of being overwhelmed by the suffering of another. Thus we avoid people who might "bring us down" or depress our spirits. As protection from this vicarious deflation of morale, we may even muster contempt and anger for those who suffer. When the object of pity is an attachment figure, functioning as a mirror of the inner self, reminding us of the darkest "truths" of our self-constructions, the contempt and anger born of pity translates into overt abuse. This explains why the frailest and most dependent and most suffering of family members bear the greatest abuse (Gelles & Cornell, 1990).

Unlike pity, compassion functions as an emotional regulator incompatible with contempt and anger. Although pity may motivate prosocial behavior with dysphoric "punishment" (to be avoided simply by withdrawing from the object of pity), compassion motivates prosocial behavior for the "reward," of understanding, emotional inter-regulation, and the hope of changing the meaning (not necessarily the circumstance) that causes the psychological harm.

"Compassion," as used in the Compassion Workshop, differs from *empathy* in depth and intensity. Empathy is identification with whatever feelings a person is experiencing, whereas compassion sees through the defenses and symptoms of anger, anxiety, emotional withdrawal, and manipulation, to the core hurts causing the defenses. Traditional therapeutic exercises to increase empathy, such as role reversals or other forms of "putting yourself in his or her shoes" may help abusers deflect their abuse or simply withdraw from the persons they would otherwise abuse. But only compassion will heal the intrapsychic hurt that causes abuse. Only compassion can repair and enhance the attachment bond.

A GENERIC TREATMENT FOR ATTACHMENT ABUSE

The internal mechanism of self-building is so fundamental a function of the attachment bond that it is possible to develop a generic treatment to alter the dysfunctions of self-building common to all forms of attachment abuse, perpetrated by all descriptions of abusers. The Compassion Workshop was developed for spouse, child, and elder-parent abusers of all ages, genders, sexual orientations, races, and socioeconomic classes. The Manual included in this publication was prepared for use with spouse/lover abusers. (The core of the treatment is easily adapted to child and elder abusers.) The pilot project to develop the treatment was conducted on male, predominantly heterosexual spouse abusers, in a field experiment with random assignment of 100 subjects to experimental and standard agency treatment groups. The purpose of this research was to develop the treatment, hence the results of the experiment can scarcely be considered a sound evaluation of the finished program. Nevertheless the data suggest that, after 1 year, the Compassion Workshop eliminated violence and verbal aggression (measured from report of *vic-*

tims) at a much greater rate than the standard treatments at five different community mental health centers. The treatment also greatly increased well-being and compassion for spouse and reduced anger–hostility and anxiety at a much greater rate than standard agency treatment.

CHAPTER SUMMARY

This brief chapter introduced the major issues raised by a new treatment for intimate abusers. The Compassion Workshop emphasizes the critical importance of the self-building function of the attachment bond. This unique self-building capacity makes attachment relationships the most significant force in the development of an individual's sense of self. As the salient attachment emotion, compassion instills the capacity for self-regulation and self-control necessary for moral agency. Repair and enhancement of the self-building functions of the attachment bond seem requisite to successful treatment of attachment abusers. Because the emphasis of this approach falls on building skill in the regulation of one of the most basic of emotional mechanisms, a generic treatment, emphasizing self-compassion and compassion for loved ones, emerges as the core of interventions to relieve all forms of attachment disorders, before they ever lead to abuse and violence.

2 The Experience of Attachment

Attachment is the psychobiological glue that holds the family together and maintains its function as the structural foundation of society. The father of attachment theory, British developmental psychiatrist, John Bowlby, describes his work as:

> a way of conceptualizing the propensity of human beings to make strong affectional bonds to particular others and of explaining the many forms of emotional distress and personality disturbances, including anxiety, anger, depression, and emotional detachment, to which unwilling separation and loss give rise. (p. 127, 1977)

ATTACHMENT AND SURVIVAL

Attachment theory began as a variant of object relations (Bowlby, 1988). Both theoretical approaches describe human beings as seeking attachment from birth, an hypothesis well supported by the work of Daniel Stern on the interpersonal life of the infant (1985). Bowlby's initial departure from Kleinian object relations was the rejection of a hunger (if not pleasure) drive association with the first object: the breast. In contrast, Bowlby held that attachment motivation was independent of hunger and other drives but as necessary for survival. In support of his early position, Bowlby cited the work of Spitz (1945, 1946), whose experiment in a French foundling home saw infants succumb to anaclitic depression from the deprivation of attachment interactions, even though their physical maintenance needs were met. Harlow's (1959) famous experiment with monkeys, who preferred a cloth mother that gave no food to a nourishing wire mother, was also cited, along with the work of Lorenz (1963), which demonstrated that the imprinting behavior of goslings was independent of feeding.

Evolutionary considerations add a survival explanation of the strong attachment bond observed in human beings. The relatively long period of total dependence of human offspring on care givers necessitated a powerful internal motivation to attach. There were also formidable motivations in the unforgiving environment of early humans. Lacking claws, sharp teeth, speed, agility, and strength, early humans could only compete with other predators (while precariously avoiding the status of prey) by forming social units to fight cooperatively. Note that social cooperation comes *after* the establishment of the attachment bond. The strength of our capacity to form attachment bonds is not only how we survived as a species but *why* we survived. In that sense, civilization can be described as a by-product of the attachment bond.

THE EXPERIENCE OF ATTACHMENT

The phenomenology of attachment relationships divides into two broad categories. Bowlby describes *secure* attachment as the result of meeting the child's affectional needs, which permits the child to explore the environment with the assurance of a safe return at any time for comfort and protection. *Insecure* attachment, thought to arise from (a) inconsistent parental response to the child's care-soliciting behaviors, (b) invalidation of the child's explorational attempts, (c) rejection of the child's need for love and acceptance, is characterized by shame, rejection-anxiety, and simultaneous fear of, and longing for, close relationships.

A number of empirical studies, most notably by Ainsworth and her colleagues (1978, 1985), have explored *patterns* of attachment, using a method known as "Strange Situation." In these studies, infants and toddlers were faced with incremental challenges (encountering a stranger, being left alone with strangers, and so on), ending with reunion with the mother. The child's behavior when reunited with the mother reveals the pattern of attachment. Ainsworth used the data from these studies to consolidate the classification of secure attachment and to subdivide that of insecure attachment in the following way.

In the *anxious avoidant condition,* the child shows conspicuous avoidance of, and inattention to the mother when she returns (even though heart-rate recordings indicate considerable emotional distress). If picked up by the mother, the child does not cling and avoids eye contact or interaction. The avoidant child has already learned to suppress powerful feelings. He or she expresses feelings indirectly and avoids physical contact when the need for contact seems the greatest.

In the *anxious resistant* or *ambivalent condition,* the child displays anger and ambivalence at the mother's return, alternating between seeking and resisting contact. If picked up, he or she soon wants to be released. When released, he or she soon signals a desire to be picked up. This child is quick to become disorganized, with a poor ability to regain equilibrium. Possessed of an apparent low threshold for the stress of separation, the child remains difficult to comfort.

In the *securely attached condition,* the child immediately seeks contact with the mother and maintains proximity to her, sometimes exhibiting emotional release through brief "protest." However, the child clings securely if picked up and is easily comforted. After a brief time he or she is likely to become rapidly reorganized and demonstrate an interest in play. The child expresses feelings directly, always in proportion to the stressor, and then easily regains equilibrium.

Patterns of attachment, once established, tend to persist (Sroufe, 1984, 1985), forming the basis of stable personality traits, often called, *attachment style*. The *securely attached* individual knows that attachment figures will be available, responsive, and helpful when needed. The *anxious resistant* or *ambivalent* individual is uncertain whether attachment figures will be available and helpful if called on. The *anxious avoidant* individual expects to be rejected (Bowlby, 1988).

West and Sheldon (1988) identify four clinical conditions based on insecure attachment style: *compulsive self-reliance, compulsive care giving, compulsive care seeking*, and *angry withdrawal*. Clinicians can easily locate most attachment abusers within these categories.

It should be noted that attachment styles are probably greatly influenced by temperament. Kagan (1989), for example, points out that the young child's temperamental tendency to become anxious and fearful or remain spontaneous in unfamiliar situations can affect classification of attachment style by the Strange Situation protocol. Cultural differences in socialization may also play a part in how infants are classified, as suggested by a German study in which the children seemed to present greater control of anxiety as some reflection of cultural values (Grossman, Grossman, Huber, & Wartner, 1981). No doubt temperament and cultural socialization play some important part in how we understand attachment styles. They may even set the parameters of variation for the enormously influential role that parent–child interactions play in building the emerging self of the child. But from a clinical point of view, particularly when treating adults with attachment deficits, a precise parceling of which variance is due to purely attachment style, temperament, and cultural socialization is unnecessary, if we allow the construct of attachment style the umbrella status for what, after years of interaction, is probably a family of inseparable developmental influences. The construct of attachment style, though not as pure as researchers would like, will prove resiliently useful to the clinician's task of relieving pain.

THE PSYCHOBIOLOGY OF ATTACHMENT

Hundreds of lyrics of popular songs seem to have been way ahead of research into the psychobiology of attachment. Consider phrases that describe the *pavement always staying beneath his feet before*, but now he shouts, *all at once am I several stories high*, but when he *lost his baby he almost lost his mind*, cause he can't *eat or sleep or drink or think, can't do nothin' but shake* without her. Popular wisdom has always held that love is like an addiction and that losing attachment figures is like drug withdrawal syndrome. Now there is empirical evidence. The endogenous opiate system seems, indeed, to provide a pleasure reward for attachment and a withdrawal penalty for loss of the attachment bond (van der Kolk, 1989). Although this line of research is primarily confined to laboratory rodents and nonhuman primates for ethical reasons, the evidence includes structural changes in the number of opioid receptors in the cingulate gyrus of mice deprived of care giving in the first few weeks of life (Bonnet, Miller, & Simon, 1976). The separation distress of baby monkeys *and* the maternal response to them have been greatly reduced through the administration of morphine (Newman, Murphy, & Harbough, 1982; Panksepp, 1982; Panksepp, Najam, & Soares, 1979; Panksepp, Sivey, & Normansell, 1985). The interruption of the attachment bond caused by drugs may explain how addicted mothers can abandon their infants with scarcely a tinge of regret.

Panksepp (1989) has postulated a localized brain system for separation distress and panic, which seems to mediate the attachment/separation response. We may yet find that attachment/separation information is processed in a separate neural network, much like information about pain (Ornstein & Sobel, 1990).

Other investigations have linked separation from attachment figures to immunocompetence (Notarious & Herrick, 1989). Kiecolt-Glaser et al. (1987) demonstrate that the more recent the separation and the stronger the attachment feelings of divorced women, the weaker their defenses against bacterial and viral infection. Compared to a sample of married women, the recently separated/divorced women showed lower percentages of helper T lymphocytes (which stimulate the antibodies that ward off infection) and weaker control of virus latency. James Lynch (1990), in a review of the effects of a broken heart on illness, suggests that the absence of an attachment relationship greatly increases the risk of all major causes of death.

The mounting psychobiological evidence merely confirms common parlance about attachment relationships as addictive ("Can't live without her,"), characterized by withdrawal symptoms as a result of separation ("It's like a part of me was torn out when she left,"), and by ill-health consequences of separation ("He's sick with a broken heart").

ATTACHMENT AND SELF-CONSTRUCTION

The term, "*self-construction*" is a rubric for a set of beliefs, feelings, and behaviors about the self that form the perspective from which individuals construct meaning. *Self-constructions make up the unique lens through which each individual sees the world.* In fact, the brain processes information about the world—gives it *meaning*—according to how it constructs the self. For example, moving across the room *means* something different to the person who cannot walk than to the person who walks with ease. Likewise, emotional interaction with an attachment figure *means* something different to a person who gives love freely than to one who believes love to be hurtful or his own love to be inadequate or damaging to others.

Another point about neural processing might further illuminate the role of self-constructions in determining what the world means to an individual. Most of what the brain does in the realm of information processing is select what to process and thereby filter out what not to process. Trillions of bits of information confront the senses at any instant in time; the brain must use an organizing method to select from the chaos of stimuli and to process the selected data into meaningful constructions. To borrow an example from Ornstein and Sobel (1987), the brain formulates the sensory data stimulated by massive slabs of concrete, steel, and glass glittering with sunlight, into the coherent image of a skyscraper, whether or not it has prior experience of skyscrapers. For the brain's delimiting function to run smoothly, it must have certain rules of what to process and what to ignore. Those rules are partly written by experience, but fundamentally determined by an individual's self-constructions. *Individuals construct the world in accordance with their self-constructions.* Understand a person's self-constructions and you know that person's construction of the world, and vice versa. *If I construe myself to be unlovable, incompetent, or nonempathic, I will construct a painful world replete with confirmation, while ignoring evidence to the contrary.* Relevant to clinical practice, empirical evidence for selective processing emerges from the negative bias thinking of depressed subjects, documented by Beck and his associates (1979).

Figure 2.1 suggests how the brain goes about selecting certain data and filtering out others. The brain constructs a certain meaning, heavily influenced by past experience and by constructions of self, and then forces the selected data and the internal construction to fit together. It's as if mental feelers were radiated from the brain to select which data in the outside world will form the best fit with the internal construction of meaning. The selection of validating data from the external world and the fit between the selected data and the internal construction of meaning may be diffuse and incoherent, solid and flexible, or narrow and rigid, depending on the organization of an individual's self-constructions.

Relationships with attachment figures determine the development of a child's self-constructions and provide them with continuous confirmation and reinforcement. The child's self-constructions in turn determine how the child sees the world and how the inner self of the child becomes organized (Guidano, 1987; Guidano & Liotti, 1983).

Self-constructions affect attachment style by virtue of what Bowlby (1973) called "internal working models." These

Figure 2.1 Constructions of meaning.

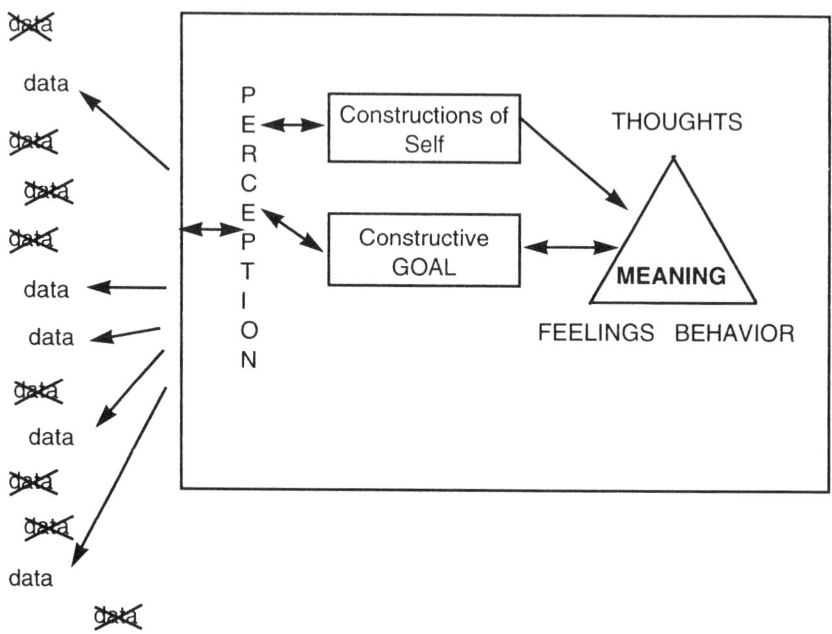

have two important features that determine whether the self is worthy of love *and* whether attachment figures will be loving and responsive (Bowlby, 1973), that is, they tell us how much love we deserve and how much we can expect others to give. In that sense, they are interactive constructions of self and others. Main, Kaplan, and Cassidy (1985) define the internal working model as, "A set of conscious and/or unconscious rules for the organization of information relevant to attachment . . . experiences, feelings, and ideations" (p. 66).

Empirical support for internal working models as determinants of attachment style has been strongest for the ambivalent style of attachment, which produces negative views of self (Cassidy, 1988; Kaplan & Main, 1985; Main, Kaplan, & Cassidy, 1985). The attachment styles of toddlers have been linked convincingly to social and emotional adjustment and maladjustment throughout early childhood (e.g., Bretherton, 1985).

The lifelong continuity of internal working models has been widely tested in adults. For example, the childhood attachment styles of mothers predict both the quality of their interactions with their own children *and* the security of their children's attachment (Crowell & Feldman, 1987; Fish, 1993; Grossman, Fremmer-Bombik, Rudolf & Grossman, 1988; Main et al., 1985). Hazan and Huth (1993) found that stability of internal working models outweighed change by 78% to 22%.

Research has shown further that people with a secure attachment style tend to view themselves as relatively undistressed and others as supportive. Those with an avoidant attachment style view the self as undistressed but see others as unreliable and unresponsive. Persons with an ambivalent attachment style tend to view the self as distressed and others as responsive (Kobak & Sceery, 1988).

Supported by the perdurable nature of attachment styles, the construct of internal working models sheds light on what we know of romantic love. For instance, compared to those with secure attachment styles, insecurely attached persons report more negative experiences of love, have a history of shorter romantic relationships, hold more negative beliefs about love, and provide bleaker descriptions of their childhood relationships with parents (Collins & Read, 1990; Hazan & Shaver, 1987). They also suffer more virulent self-doubt and less self-perceived acceptability to others (Feeney & Noller, 1990; Hazan & Shaver, 1987).

As any clinician can attest, there is not always congruence between how one constructs the self as an attachment figure and how one constructs others. Bartholomew and Horowitz (1991) have developed a more versatile four-category model of adult attachment styles that is sensitive to independent variance in assessment of self and others. In this model, those with a *secure* attachment style experience the self as worthy of love and expect that other people will be generally accepting and responsive; "I'm lovable and you will find my love worth having." Persons with a *preoccupied* attachment style view the self as unworthy of love, but hold great value for others. "I'm not lovable, but you're so loving that I'll do anything to get you to stay with me." These individuals become preoccupied with relationships as a measure of self-worth. Holding the self as unworthy and others as rejecting, those with an *avoidant* attachment style eschew close relationships; "I'm unlovable and you'll reject me anyway, so why bother." Those with a *dismissing* attachment style apparently feel worthy of love, but hold a negative disposition of others, which makes them dismissing of attachment relationships; "I'm lovable, but you're either too insensitive to see it or you're just not worthy of my love." Although the majority of people seem to hold congruent constructions of self and others, two classifications, the *preoccupied* and *dismissing,* represent significant disparity between constructions of self and potential attachment figures. They also constitute two distinct coping strategies. In the preoccupied style, people blame *themselves* for perceived rejections by others. They are able, therefore, to maintain a positive view of others, at the cost of an ever-eroding view of self. In the dismissing attachment style, people downplay the importance of others whom they have experienced as rejecting, and are thereby able to maintain high (if ultimately shallow) self-esteem, as long as they avoid attachment relationships (Bartholomew & Horowitz, 1991).

ATTACHMENT AND SELF-ORGANIZATION

"*Self-organization*" refers to how the inner experience of the self forms coherent streams of meaning. In other words, self-organization makes the self, with its repertoire of familiar thoughts, feelings, and behaviors, make sense to the individual. This is what we mean by statements such as:

> "Work brings out the real me."
> "I wasn't myself when I said that."
> "It's not like me to feel like this."

When self-organization functions well, we feel whole, complete, and secure. When it does not, we feel empty, incomplete, or inadequate.

Infant and child research has demonstrated that attachment figures play a basic role in the development of an individual's self-organization (Bell & Ainsworth, 1972; Bowlby, 1969, 1977, 1980, 1984; Brazelton, Koslowski, & Main, 1974; Guidano, 1987, 1991; Main et al., 1985). Many theoreticians and researchers have extended the concept of self-organizational development through the life span (e.g., Ainsworth, 1989; Bowlby, 1988; Field, 1985; Kegan, 1982; Lyddon & Alford, 1993; West & Sheldon, 1988), suggesting that people, throughout their lives, construct and organize the self to accommodate feedback about the self from attachment figures.

This organizational accommodation takes place predominantly through inter-regulation of emotional experience, first emerging in the early parent–infant dyad, through which children learn the process of self-regulation (Klinnert & Binghman, 1994). Inter-regulation reaches a zenith of emotional experience in what Daniel Stern (1985) calls, "attunement" between parent and child. Tiffany Field (1985) also uses this wonderful term in her explanation:

> Attachment might . . . be viewed as a relationship that develops between two or more organisms as their behavioral and physiological systems become attuned to each other. Each partner provides meaningful stimulation for the other and has a modulating influence on the other's arousal level. The relationship facilitates an optimal growth state that is threatened by changes in the individuals or their relationship or by separation and the behavioral and physiological disorganization that ensue. Thus, attachments are psychobiological(ly) adaptive for the organization, equilibrium, and growth of the organism. Because the organism's behavioral repertoire, physiological makeup, and growth needs are an integrated multivariate complex that changes developmentally, multiple and different types of attachments are experienced across the life span. (Field, 1985, pp. 415–416)

In other words, the process of attachment, in stimulating the organization (and reorganization) of the self to accommodate emotional bonding with another, is *self-building*. Perhaps the greatest psychological reward of attachment is its *enhancement* of self-organization, of helping one to *feel whole.* Once again, the mechanism by which attachment seems to provide this subjective feeling of wholeness is the modulating effect of attachment relationships on the internal arousal level of participants. Thus the distressed child is calmed and comforted by a nurturing parent, and the bored child is aroused by the teaching parent.

In fact, children *need* to have their feelings regulated by attachment figures (or at least someone playing that role for them). Distressed infants cry until exhausted or until comforted by caretakers. Anxious children need to be calmed and made to feel safe and secure. Frightened children need to be hugged and comforted by adults whom they feel are smarter, more powerful, and able to protect them. There is substantial psychological reward for both the child recipient of emotional regulation and the parent who renders it. That reward, after all, must be sufficient to help us endure, even to some extent enjoy, the many hardships of caring for helpless children.

In the course of normal development, children gradually learn to regulate their own internal experience, including their feelings. For an example of how this process works, consider the child's experience of hunger. The maturing child learns that the uncomfortable feeling of hunger is relieved, not by the caretaker providing food, but the by the child eating the food. Eating, which the child controls, in turn controls the unpleasant experience of hunger. Thus children learn that regulation of internal experience falls within their power. They become skilled in self-regulation. They develop constructive schemata of self-regulation.

The mechanism for developing self-regulatory schemata is, once again, the emotional modulation and attunement that characterize attachment relationships. Unfortunately, this mechanism is biased toward negative feelings, which carry more urgent survival messages than positive ones. Anger, fear, and anxiety are especially powerful emotional modulators among the parties of attachment relationships. Young children do not know what to fear or worry about or avoid or fight. To pick up signals of threat or danger, they must attune their internal experience to that of their attachment figures. Thus the self-regulatory skill they develop is profoundly influenced by the degree of self-regulatory skill exhibited by their parents. This is why anxious and depressed parents tend to raise anxious and depressed children. Add to this persistent negative information about the status of the self as a loving and lovable attachment figure, and the child develops severe deficits in affect-regulation.

ATTACHMENT EMOTIONS

Several emotions are associated with the establishment, maintenance, and reinstatement of attachment bonds (Table 2.1). Each shares in the survival-based drive that gives meaning to attachment relationships.

The emotional rewards of establishing attachment relationships are among the highest available in human experience: interest, compassion, trust, and love. So it is no sur-

Table 2.1 The Range of Emotions from Attachment to Detachment

Attachment emotions	*Threats to attachment*	*Motivation to reattach*	*If reattachment fails or is expected to fail*	*Detachment*
Interest	Loss of interest	Guilt	Anger	Depression
Compassion	Lack of compassion	Shame		Despair
Trust	Lack of Trust	Fear of abandonment		Bitterness
Love	Loss of love Fear of engulfment			Numbness

prise that *threats to attachment* loom in loss of interest, lack of compassion, diminishment of trust, fear of engulfment, and waning love. In turn, these stimulate three of the most painful feelings in human experience: shame, guilt, and abandonment-anxiety. These punitive feelings serve both as deterrents to damaging the attachment bond and incentives to *reattach* or reinstate a suspended or diminished attachment bond. In so doing, each serves a separate intrapsychic as well as interpersonal function.

The customary distinction between shame and guilt centers on the difference between the self and behavior. For empirical reviews of guilt and shame, see Baumeister, Stillwell & Heatherton, 1994; Tangney, 1990, 1991). We feel guilt over what we *do* and shame over what we *are*. Thus *shame* occurs when one feels:

- uninteresting (or unattractive)
- unworthy of compassion
- untrustworthy
- unlovable or loving inadequately (e.g., one's love is insufficient to stop the abuse of an attachment figure).

In other words, we feel *shame* over our defective or inadequate status as loving and lovable persons. On the other hand, *guilt* occurs when one feels:

- uninterested in an attachment figure
- not compassionate to an attachment figure
- not trusting or betraying trust
- not loving enough.

Either guilt or shame will activate fear of abandonment (also known as rejection anxiety or abandonment anxiety or abandonment terror), creating a powerful inner motivation to *reattach*. Shame, guilt, and fear of abandonment often interact and coalesce into a feeling that might be called *self-ache*. This can be experienced as a sense of emptiness, lack of purpose, or an undifferentiated longing, coming in giant waves of affect or in a quiet, dull, persistent ache.

The interpersonal function of the reattachment emotions hinges on the outward manifestations of shame, guilt, and abandonment anxiety. If perceived as sincerely felt, these will prompt the withdrawing attachment figure to reattach. (If you need to be convinced of this, try to imagine something more pathetic than a child experiencing shame, of feeling utterly bad about himself. You will feel a strong desire to embrace the child and tell him that everything is okay, that *he's* okay.) For shame, guilt, and abandonment anxiety to prompt reinstatement of the attachment bond, their punitive power must seem sufficient to preclude future transgressions. The offended attachment figure needs to know that the emotional price of attacks on the attachment bond ensures future protection of it.

If preservation and reinstatement of the attachment bond are the natural and healthy functions of shame, guilt, and fear of abandonment, why do they so often become distorted and unhealthy? The answer rings sadly familiar to most clinicians. When manipulated early in life, not to preserve or reinstate the attachment bond, but to control the autonomy and individual development of the child, shame, guilt, and abandonment anxiety are stimulated by normal, healthy desires for independence, autonomy, privacy, even the very sense of self. Sensitivity to this sort of invasiveness produces a powerful fear of engulfment, of being overwhelmed by one's own feelings stimulated by another. It is why some people become furious when a "guilt trip is laid on" them. It is one common reason why a great many people fear intimacy.

When *reattachment fails*, or is *expected to fail*, or when tolerance to shame and guilt is so low as to require instant relief, *anger* emerges to reinstate the attachment bond through stimulation of shame, guilt, and abandonment anxiety in the attachment partner. But anger has a prior and much more urgent function that undermines this purpose. Anger powers the defense of the attachment bond from *outside* threats. Few human experiences can match the power of the anger provoked when an attachment figure is physically attacked, or the jealous rage when a lover strays.

The problem with anger in attachment relationships is that the perceived attacker is not an outside threat, but a loved one, for *anger makes enemies of the beloved.* The anger stimulated by perceived assaults on the attachment bond only does more damage to the very prize it would protect, stimulating torrents of shame, guilt, and abandonment anxiety, that in turn stimulate more anger, in a kind of relentless pendulum of pain, described in more detail in the next chapter.

When the attachment bond finally crumbles under assault of the pendulum of pain, a period of *detachment* occurs, featuring depression, despair, bitterness, and numbness. Dread of detachment may be the throbbing wound at the heart of attachment abuse, as we shall see in the next chapter.

CHAPTER SUMMARY

Attachment is the psychobiological glue that holds the family together and maintains its function as the structural foundation of society. An innate survival-based drive, attachment is independent of, and of parallel importance to, other biological drives. Patterns of attachment, established in early childhood, tend to persist throughout life, unless altered through intervention. Attachment relationships play a self-building role in creating constructions of self and in organizing the individual's sense of self. (Together, these act as the lens through which the world is viewed and the organizing method by which meaning is constructed.) Modulation and interregulation of emotions form the physiological mechanism through which attachment relationships build the self. Children learn to regulate their internal experience through this interregulatory process, which creates within the child self-regulatory schemata. But the range, efficiency, and flexibility of the developing schemata can be greatly impaired by the range, efficiency, and limitations of the regulatory skills to which they become attuned, namely those of their attachment figures. Powerful positive emotions help to establish and maintain attachment relationships: interest, compassion, trust, and love. More powerful negative emotions provide motivation to maintain or reinstate damaged or suspended attachment bonds: shame, guilt, and fear of abandonment. When persistent anger enters the swirl of attachment emotions, the culture of abuse is fertilized and ripened to yield its harvest of pain.

Note to the Reader

Intended for practicing clinicians, this book cannot hope to do justice to the varied and emerging field of research into the ramifications of attachment theory. Fortunately, recent books by Sperling and Berman (1994) and West and Sheldon-Keller (1994) review the empirical evidence, theoretical issues, and methodological considerations involved in applying attachment theory to adults.

3 Attachment Abuse: Why We Hurt the Ones We Love

In the last chapter it was argued that self-constructions determine what sort of information the brain will process and how it will process it. In no area of human endeavor is this more true than in attachment relationships. Our constructions of those we love are so interwoven with constructions of self, that almost everything we do with (or to) attachment figures reflects deeper constructions of self. If constructions of self are fraught with doubts and fear of inadequacy, especially concerning one's ability to love and be loved, some degree of abuse is almost assured. The inability to stop a child from crying or a frail elder parent from brooding is likely to be construed by abusers as the inadequacy of their personal significance, indeed, of their lovableness and the value of their love.

Also in the last chapter, the effects of attachment relationships on self-organization were discussed. Because the capacity to form viable attachment bonds is greatly influenced by how an individual's sense of self is organized, a few more points about the relevance of self-organization to negotiating attachment relationships need to be made.

Self-organization accounts for the continuity of life, by shaping perceptions, sensations, thoughts, emotions, and behavior into coherent streams of meaning. As a result of this unending process of *meaning making*, life by and large makes sense to us. When the meaning-making process functions well, we experience life as whole persons and present to the outside world as full and rich personalities. We perform at our highest levels, achieve optimum growth, and enjoy enriched relationships.

But when the meaning-making system of self functions poorly, we feel disjointed, impulsive, chaotic, uncentered, even fragmented, unsure of ourselves, anxious, angry, and depressed, as we construct conflictive and unrealistic streams of meaning. Certain individuals respond to this experience of internal chaos with an iron-handed, repressive style of self-management. Expecting their needs for support and intimacy to result in disappointment or rejection and pain, they deny their most humane attachment desires altogether, in classical adherence to the anxious avoidant pattern of attachment. To maintain this disregard of their internal reality, they necessarily become narrow and rigid in self-organization.

Table 3.1 depicts self-organization as a continuum, with diffusion and rigidity at either extreme. People with diffuse self-organization may try to re-formulate the self to conform to attachment figures' projected images and expectations, whether realistic or idealized, rewarding or damaging. Persons with rigid self-organization try to make their attachment figures match projected images of self, whether realistic or idealized. In the optimal middle ground of this continuum, one retains maximal individual integrity and respect for the individual integrity of attachment figures, while enhancing the self through affectional bonds with attachment figures.

Attachment abusers fall on either end of the self-organization continuum. In either extreme, the attachment figure, serving as an imperfect mirror of the inner self, presents the never-satisfying illusion of self-control through manipulation of the mirror. *The abuser feels compelled to manipulate the attachment figure to bring about a tolerable inner experience of self.*

Attachment abuse is hurting the feelings or the body of an attachment figure to construct a more tolerable, if momentary, experience of the self. In this functional definition

Table 3.1 Continuum of Self-Organization: Cognitive–Affective–Behavioral and Attachment Styles

Diffuse self-organization	*Optimal self-organization*	*Rigid self-organization*
Conflictive cognitive schemata, inconsistent meaning making, confusion	Integrated schemata, consistent, varied meaning, clarity of thinking, tolerance of ambiguity	Narrow range of schemata—only one "right" way; closed to new information
Anxious or depressed, empty, incomplete, not genuine	Adaptive and flexible, growth oriented, never feels phoney or unreal	Constricted affect or obsessive or compulsive
Impulsive, erratic behavior or avoidant inaction	Wide repertoire of appropriate behaviors	Repetitive behavior, over-controlled
Insecure attachments, fear of abandonment, fear of engulfment	Secure attachments	Insecure, ambivalent attachments, fear of abandonment, engulfment
Attachment figures needed to feel whole	Attachment figures generally enhance experience without affecting integrity of self-organization	Attachment figures must conform to projected self-image and expectancies
If pathological, borderline, dependent, passive-aggressive, or avoidant personalities, dissociative disorders	Not pathological	If pathological, narcissistic, paranoid, obsessive-compulsive personality disorders

lies the key to successful treatment of abusers, who must be trained in more viable ways to construct a consistently tolerable experience of self.

ABUSE AND THE NEED FOR EXTERNAL REGULATION

In the last chapter, we discussed how attachment relationships provide a mechanism for the developing child to learn self-regulation of external experience. For many complex reasons, some adults never develop the capacity to consistently regulate internal experience. They need someone else to calm them when they are anxious, to comfort them when they're hurt or frightened, to dissipate their depression, and to make them feel secure when their sense of self is weakened. They usually take these needs to the nearest adults, or, in the worst case, to their own children. The requests they make of attachment figures constitutes far more than a need for emotional support in a crisis or a desire to be "cheered up" by a friend or lover when feeling down. For these individuals feel "incomplete" without someone else to regulate their feelings—to "make me feel right," to "make me feel good," to provide "the security I need." *Attachment abuse begins with the abuser's need for someone else to relieve the fear of being overwhelmed by his feelings and the need for someone else to set limits on his feelings.* Note that for some abusers, who have encapsulated their emotional repertoire, feeling anything at all may invoke fear of an overwhelming flood of affect.

As long as another person is *needed* to regulate one's feelings, an adult relationship of equal emotional exchange seems impossible. More likely, interactions will languish on the emotional level of child-to-adult. The inevitable imbalance of emotional power in such relationships, whether or not they are abusive, has much to do with the difficulty of one or both parties in regulating internal experience.

Though always dysfunctional, emotional dependence becomes abusive when anger serves simultaneously to numb internal pain *and* to blame the attachment figure who is expected to provide external relief of pain. Note that this blame has nothing to do with the cause of pain. The mere failure to take away the abuser's pain, even when its cause is not remotely connected to the victim, is sufficient to merit punishment in this twisted logic of the heart. A deep experience of powerlessness by both parties is the inexorable price of emotional dependence.

ATTACHMENT ABUSE AND THE PENDULUM OF PAIN

Before reaching the detachment phase, many relationships endure a long and painful pendular ride between *anger*, on the one extreme, and anxious renewal of the attachment bond on the other (see Figure 3.1).

The pendular swing begins when anger, stimulated by failures to reattach, resolves into still more shame, guilt, and abandonment anxiety, shifting the pendulum once again toward *reattachment*. However, if attempts to reattach are powered more by the need for *relief of pain* than a genuine rekindling of interest, compassion, trust, and love (as they almost always are in abusive relationships), the attempts at reattachment will again founder on the rocky terrain of *threats to attachment*, only to swing back, once again, through the pain of shame–guilt–abandonment anxiety, to the anger side of the pendular arc. This hellish ride back and

Figure 3.1 The pendulum of pain.

forth will continue until both parties, out of exhaustion, simply *detach* from one another, and either find new attachments or face a period of depression, despair, bitterness, and numbness.

Anger also plays a tactical role in attachment relationships, although this is secondary to its role as stimulant and pain reliever within the individual. Some people use anger to withdraw from the attachment bond, if not *sever* it, at least temporarily: "Just leave me alone! I can't stand to be around you," they shout, stomping out of the room.

Others use anger to assault the defenses of the withdrawing partner, in the hope of stimulating shame and guilt, which may then lead to reinstatement of the attachment bond. Anger is also used in misguided attempts to stimulate a renewal of compassion in the attachment figure: "I want her to be hurt so she'll understand how I feel."

Of course, the hope of forcing the lover to understand goes awry, due to the natural response when confronted with the anger of another—defensive anger—which is incompatible with compassion.

In any case, the degree of anger within the attachment relationship relates to expectations of failure to maintain or renew the attachment bond. Individually, the habitually angry person, like the detached person who has given up, feels defective as an attachment figure and inadequate as a lovable and loving person.

ANGER OVER DENIED ATTACHMENT ENTITLEMENT

Anger over denied entitlement, that is, not getting the reward, special treatment, or privileged consideration to which a person feels entitled, is not infrequently related to self-perceived defectiveness as a lovable and loving person: "I don't get the love I should get, therefore, I should get some special privileges." Or, "It's so hard being me, I deserve special consideration."

Certainly not all anger over entitlement is so directly related to attachment deficits. As we'll see in a later chapter, anger addiction—a condition in which the brain continually looks for reasons to be angry—contributes a great deal to the entitlement–anger connection. Yet it is hard to imagine finding an anger-addicted person who does not suffer from self-perceived defectiveness as a lovable and loving person.

ABUSER CHARACTERISTICS THAT CONTRIBUTE TO ABUSE

Two salient attributes of abusers—attachment deficits and poor affect regulation—loom as utterly crucial to attachment abuse. Other prominent characteristics, which can act as impediments to successful treatment, seem to be contributors to, or effects of, these two interrelated and pervasive variables.

Figure 3.2 suggests a causal chain that leads to attachment abuse. Insufficient or inconsistent nurturing produce deficits in the self-building function of attachment relationships. These often result in distorted self-constructions and either diffuse or narrow and rigid self-organization, which, in turn, produces deficient skill in affect regulation. Deficiencies in affect regulation produce an experience of powerlessness and feeling out of control of one's internal experience. The feeling of precarious inner control intensifies the poor sense of self, which, in turn, exacerbates the negative affect unleashed by an out-of-control internal state. Poor affect regulation will drive the abuser to look outside the self for regulation. This produces external locus of control and external attributions of causality for one's behavior. (She made me do it!) The continual threat of being overwhelmed by feelings is often numbed by alcohol and drugs. It is important to note that the alcohol and drugs are a response to the out-of-control feeling that leads to abuse, not a cause of it. (Of course, alcohol and drugs can intensify this lack of control by dulling inhibitions and blurring the effects of whatever cognitive regulators the abuser may possess.)

Figure 3.2 Abuser characteristics that lead to attachment abuse.

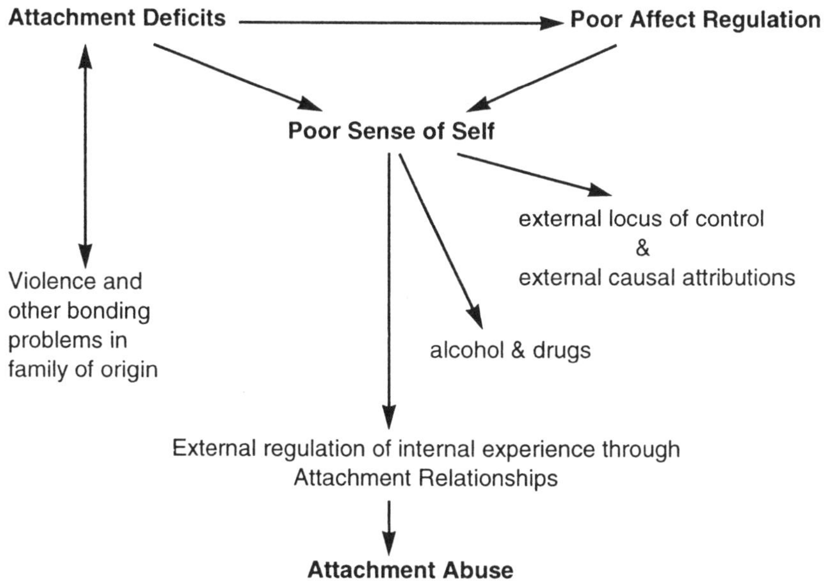

A more common source of regulation outside the self comes from attachment figures—the lover or child who makes me feel whole. But as we have seen, dependence on attachment figures for internal regulation only exacerbates the feeling of powerlessness that gnaws at abusers. External causal attributions lead abusers to blame feelings of powerlessness on attachment figures. From such blame it is but a tiny step to abuse.

The rest of this chapter cites empirical evidence for the contributors to attachment abuse. Evidence for the major causes—attachment deficits and poor affect regulation—is presented in the next chapter.

Violence in the Family of Origin

The link between violence in the family of origin and violence against one's attachment figures in adulthood has been well-established in the empirical literature. Children facing the frequent stimulation of survival-level feelings face profound developmental influences on the quality of attachment skills, self-knowledge as a potential attachment figure for others, and level of skill in negative affect-regulation. Other factors have been shown to affect parental bonding and, by implication, the development of attachment skills. These include: parental alcoholism, death of a parent, parental absence, neglect, prolonged physical illness, and mental illness (Berk, 1989). Stosny (1994) found that 80% of abusers reported at least one such problem.

Alcohol and Drug Use

In our experience with the Compassion Workshops, substance abuse has not been an obstacle to successful treatment, even though more than a third of those entering treatment have alcohol or drug-abuse problems. The notion of the abuser acting in a drunken stupor has been challenged by recent research (for a review, see Conner & Ackerley, 1994). Chronic alcoholism rather than acute intoxication on the part of the perpetrator is a better predictor of abuse (Leonard, Brommet, Parkinson, Day, & Ryan, 1985; Van Hasselt, Morrison, & Bellock, 1985). Other research suggests that alcohol use might be an excuse for violence rather than a cause (Gelles, 1974; Pagelow, 1981). Julian and McKenry (1993) saw the statistically significant predictor of alcohol abuse vanish in stepwise logistic regression analysis with perceived quality of the intimate relationship, race, and depression emerging as potent predictors. In regard to treatment, a number of researchers (e.g., Tolman & Bennett, 1990) found no evidence that alcohol and drug treatment alone is effective in reducing violence. In a controlled experiment with 106 abusers, Stosny (1994) found no interaction with alcohol use and an early version of the Compassion Workshop, that is, the amount of alcohol consumption made no difference in successful or unsuccessful response to treatment. The emotional regulation techniques taught in the Compassion Workshop offer abusers a greater control of their internal experience. We have come to an understanding that the treatment reduces a primary motivation to drink, which precedes, and usually outlasts, the effects of treatment of the addiction.

Attributions and Locus of Control

Clinicians working with attachment abusers know that the vast majority see themselves as powerless victims forced into abusive behavior. Afflicted with external locus of control and external causal attributions, abusers tirelessly blame their behavior on attachment figures or on the broad social context of the specific situations in which the abuse occurred (Bograd, 1988; Dutton, 1986; Eisikovits, Edleson, Guttmann, & Sela-Amit, 1991; Flournoy & Wilson, 1991; Holtzworth-Munroe, 1988, 1992; Rouse, 1984; Sapiente, 1988; Shields & Hanneke, 1983; Stosny, 1992; Wiehe, 1987).

Sense of Self and Self-Esteem

Virtually every published study of abusers notes their low self-esteem. Geffner and Rosenbaum (1990), Goldstein and Rosenbaum (1985), Lansky (1987), Neidig, Friedman, and Collins (1986), and Rosen (1991) have related spouse abuse to the abuser's poor sense of self. Flournoy and Wilson (1991) and Murphy (1991) found that abusers often feel inadequate and dissatisfied with themselves. Disorders of self are also found in child abusers (Conte, 1985; Overholser & Beck, 1986; Reid, Kavanagh, & Baldwin, 1987; Rogeness, Amrung, Macedo, Harris, & Fisher, 1986). Several investigators have measured abusers with psychological tests for personality disorders (Allen, Calsyn, Fehrenbach, & Benton, 1989; Barnett & Hamberger, 1992; Flournoy & Wilson, 1991; Hamberger & Hastings, 1988a, 1988b; Murphy, 1991). These studies show elevations in various subscales that indicate disturbances of personality. Yet there is far from a consensus as to whether full-blown personality disorders are prevalent in abusers, and, to whatever degree they are prevalent, whether they explain anything about the phenomenon of attachment abuse. In their 1990 review of the characteristics of abusers, Geffner and Rosenbaum reject any sort of consistent personality profile of the abuser. Other reviewers have reached the same conclusion (e.g., Berk, 1989; Gondolf, 1988; Saunders, 1987). Hart, Dutton, and Newlove, (1993), however, found that between 80%–90% of heterosexual spouse abusers suffer from some sort of personality disorder.

AGAIN, WHY WE HURT THE ONES WE LOVE

The simple answer to the question posed by this chapter goes like this: *They remind us of what we believe to be the darkest "truths" about ourselves.* The complex mechanism that gives attachment figures this power lies in the emotional-regulatory dynamic inherent in attachment relationships. Self-constructions become so intertwined with constructions of loved ones that distorted and painful self-constructions will often mislead us into thinking that we can relieve our pain by manipulating attachment figures. Diffuse or rigid organization of self-constructions will translate into impossible demands on attachment figures, with punishment for failure to meet the often outrageous demands looming as likely as it is intolerable. Reliance on attachment figures to regulate internal experience exacerbates the internal sense of powerlessness, which may find transitory relief in the exertion of power and control over loved ones. Attachment deficits (doubts about one's ability to love and be loved, to trust and be trusted, to feel compassion and be worthy of compassion, to maintain interest in another and to hold the interest of another) create deficits in affect regulation. Together, these cause a poorly integrated sense of self, which intensifies difficulties in affect regulation, which, in turn, tend to externalize locus of control and attributions of causality. These will lead to dependence on the attachment figure for regulation of internal experience. From there, the cruel step is small to attachment abuse and immersion in a pendulum of pain.

CHAPTER SUMMARY

Attachment abuse results from the abuser's inability to maintain tolerable self-constructions and his desperate illusion that manipulating the mirror-reflection provided by attachment figures will fill-in the cracks and holes in his sense of self. But the very reliance on the attachment figure for external regulation of internal experience creates a feeling of powerlessness that only aggravates the distorted sense of self causing the abuser's pain. Abusers and victims tragically get stuck in a pendulum of pain, vacillating between emotional motivations to reinstate the attachment bond and anger-driven retaliation for perceived violations against the battered attachment bond. Several characteristics of abusers contribute to the primary causal variables of attachment deficits and poor affect-regulation.

4 Pathways to Abuse: Deficits in Attachment Skills and Affect Regulation

ATTACHMENT DEFICITS

When deficits in the self-building effects of attachment relationships exist in adulthood, the afflicted parties present an impaired capacity to negotiate attachment relationships. They know searing doubts about their ability to love and be loved, to trust and be trusted, to feel compassion and be worthy of compassion, to maintain interest in another and to hold the interest of another. They want their internal experience regulated by attachment figures. They feign tolerable self-constructions by conforming to the expectations of attachment figures or by demanding that attachment figures reflect back the exact self-image they want to project. These create shallow, rocky, and treacherous waters on which to navigate relationships that are by nature most susceptible to grave damage.

Attachment in adult life is typically discussed in normative terms of relatively satisfying intimate relationships and, pathologically, in terms of interpersonal dependency, avoidance of intimacy, fear of abandonment, and jealousy (e.g., Delozier, 1982; Hindy & Schwarz, 1994; Martin, 1976; Roy, 1982; Weiss, 1982). The following pages present empirical evidence for pathological attachment styles in abusers.

While attachment variables have not been directly tested in research on elder-parent abuse, the familiar intergenerational transmission of abuse, with its profound attachment effects, is definitely at work in this area of attachment abuse (Delunas, 1990; Lau & Kosberg, 1979; Weeks, 1984). Allan (1988) found that guilt often motivates adult children to care for elder parents, establishing a common path to anger and abuse.

Not surprisingly, the child maltreatment literature has shown that attachment deficits in parents tends to produce similar deficits in their children (Berk, 1989). To a large extent, the early attachment relationship is predicted by data about parental attachment (Main, Kaplan, & Cassidy, 1985; Morris, 1981; Ricks, 1985). Parents with attachment deficits tend to lack social support systems, be more vulnerable to stress and more susceptible to disorganized family living, all factors known to contribute to child abuse (Berk, 1989). Attachment theory has been used extensively as a basis for understanding the consequences of physical child abuse (e.g., Bowlby, 1984; Egeland, Jacobvitz, & Sroufe, 1988; Egeland & Sroufe, 1981; Firestone, 1990). Main and Goldwyn (1984) were able to predict rejection of infants by the mother's representation of her own attachment history. Insecure attachment style in adulthood is significantly a product of abuse in childhood (Katsikas et al., 1993) and is sometimes more damaging than recent trauma (Gardner, 1993). Finally, Alexander (1992) has shown that sexual abuse is frequently preceded by insecure attachment.

Fear of abandonment has been associated with intimate violence by the compelling evidence that much violence occurs in the process of real or perceived relationship dissolution (Daly & Wilson, 1988; Dutton & Browning, 1988). In cases where motive could be established, Crawford and Gartner (1992) fixed actual or imminent separation in 45% of spouse murders (another 15% were motivated by jealousy, with its implicit fear of abandonment). Fear of engulfment is also a documented problem, as much violence in relationships happens at a time when the intimacy level changes direction toward more closeness (Dutton, 1988). Studies using the projective Thematic Apperception Test have found evidence of fear of abandonment and fear of intimacy (Dutton &

Browning, 1987; Dutton & Strachan, 1987). Fear of intimacy produces an almost continual anxiety, which, in abusive men, gets converted into anger. In turn, anger drives the partner further away, exacerbating the fear of abandonment and the subsequent state of anger arousal (Dutton, 1988). Probably the most compelling empirical data to date on the abandonment–engulfment roller coaster of abusive households come from the high rate of assaults on pregnant women by the prospective fathers—more than 50% of battered women are assaulted during pregnancy (U.S. Senate, 1990). Arguably, pregnancy symbolizes abandonment (in terms of its representation of a prospective rival for the affections of the attachment figure) *and* engulfment, as the pregnant lover becomes more emotionally needy.

Having linked anger, jealousy, and affective instability to the degree of emotional and physical abuse in partner relationships, Dutton (1994a) and his associates (1994) drew from Bowlby's (1969, 1973) concept of protest behavior and Bartholomew's designation of anxious-avoidant attachment as "fearful," to define a construct of "attachment-anger." Directed at a sexual partner and precipitated by perceived threats of separation or abandonment, attachment-anger and affective instability, produced by chronically frustrated attachment needs, constitute risk factors for increased abusiveness in intimate relationships. Significantly elevated anger and anxiety scores of the fearful attachment abusers led the authors to postulate that

> an emotional template of intimacy-anxiety/anger is the central affective feature of the fearful attachment pattern. . . . With the fearfully attached man, anger is an aspect of attachment independent of what transpires interpersonally, and when that anger is experienced it is both blamed and projected onto the attachment object resulting in chronic anger with that other. (Dutton, Saunders, Starzomski, & Bartholomew, 1994, p. 1380)

Hamberger and Hastings (1988a) cite the "difficulty in supporting intimacy" (p. 765) as a primary personality characteristic of abusers. In a study that used the California Psychological Inventory, a test of the normal personality, Barnett and Hamberger (1992) found abusers to differ significantly from nonviolent men "in three general areas: (a.) problems with intimacy, trust, and mutuality in relationships, (b.) impulsivity and emotional modulation, and (c.) rigid, stereotyped approaches to problem solving" (p. 25). Allen, Calsyn, Fehrenbach, and Benton (1989) found that batterers exhibited difficulties with intimacy and trust in social relationships, and tended to be aloof. Dutton (1994b) described abusers as suffering from "intimacy terror." Hale, Duckworth, Zimostrad, & Nichols (1988) found masked dependency in abusers. Flournoy and Wilson (1991) show that abusers tend to be overly dependent on their partners and ambivalent about that dependence. Murphy, Scott, Meyer, & O'Leary (1992) interpret the controlling behavior and emotional insecurity of abusers as evidence of an extreme version of the anxious avoidant style of attachment. The Murphy, Scott, Meyer, & O'Leary study (1992), with nonassaultive men experiencing marital discord and happily married men as dual comparison groups, demonstrated that assaultive men were significantly higher in levels of general vulnerability. Murphy (1991) found that abusive men were similar to happily married men on the deepness of attachments to their spouses, but differed significantly on dependency. In other words, they seem to love as much but to rely on it more. Holtzworth-Munroe and Hutchinson (1993) found that abusive men differed from nonabusive men in attributions of negative intent on the part of their wives, but only in situations that could be said to involve attachment deficits, such as rejection, jealousy, or public embarrassment by the wife. Using the Adult Attachment Interview, Young (1990) found significant differences between abusing and nonabusive men in patterns of attachment. None of the abusive men were classified as autonomous, whereas 50% of the nonabusive men in the study were so classified. Gelles (1975) and Rounsaville (1978) reported that the onset of violence began following a sudden transition in intimacy for 40% of the men who repeatedly assaulted wives. Dutton and Browning (1988) found that the quality of the intimate relationship is influenced by the male's perception of whether his partner demands too great or too little affection, attention, and emotional support. Julian and McKenry (1993) found that the male's perceived quality of the intimate relationship predicted his violence and nullified the effects of alcohol use as a predictor variable.

Although the function of compassion in attachment relationships, as discussed in this work, has not been directly studied, researchers have documented low empathy in child abusers (e.g., Wiehe, 1987), and clinicians have observed reduced degrees of empathy in spouse abusers (e.g., Gondolf, 1987; Pence & Paymar, 1993).

Widely recognized as a symptom of dysfunctional attachment, jealousy is a more elusive construct, for the measurement of which there are no widely accepted or widely used instruments (Murphy, 1991). We must rely, then, on survey measurements of less-than-perfect reliability and validity, as well as on the many clinical reports that cite some form of jealousy as a reason for abuse in as many as 90% of the reported cases (Bowker, 1983; Davidson, 1978; Follingstad et al., 1990; Hilberman & Munson, 1977–1978; Martin, 1976; Rounsaville, 1978; Roy, 1982; Stosny, 1992, 1994; Walker, 1980, 1984, 1989; White & Mullen, 1989). Another testament to the prominence of jealousy as a motivation in attachment abuse lies in the existence of whole sections on the subject appearing in most published manuals for treatment of spouse abusers (e.g., Neidig, 1991; Sonkin & Durphy, 1989; Stordeur & Stille, 1989).

Normative data adds to the chain of evidence for the relationship of violence to attachment deficits. In a survey of college students to investigate the extent to which normative attitudes condone spouse violence, Greenblat (1985) reported that both men and women rejected violence as acceptable behavior. In only one circumstance, other than self-defense, was violence deemed acceptable: in cases that threaten attachment bonds, such as coming upon one's wife while she is physically abusing their child, or catching her in bed with another man. Significantly, men and women alike saw these circumstances as justifiable causes of spouse violence.

SOCIALIZATION AND ATTACHMENT DEFICITS

The multiple-attachment deficits, poor affect regulation, violent origins, and defective sense of self suffered by many abusers make them more vulnerable to the most negative aspects of normative socialization. It has been long understood that men are socialized from an early age to engage in more aggressive play than females (Boulton, 1994), that aggression marks the school world of boys far more than girls (Weisfield, 1994), and that males are far more often the victims of harsh physical punishment (Eron & Heusmann, 1989).

Much attention has focused on the unfortunate effects of gender socialization on festering social problems, such as the inequitable division of domestic labor, decision-making authority within families, and political and economic power outside of families. But normative socialization also creates a gender gap of attachment skill and emotional power in adult relationships. The emerging literature of the men's psychology movement suggests that normative gender socialization creates attachment deficits and non-relational attitudes toward sexuality in boys and men.

> To get some idea of how gender role socialization worked, think back to how it was in your own childhood. Boys played with mechanical objects such as cars and trucks, or with very aggressive "dolls" such as military figures or super-heroes, and began to develop action-oriented attitudes, while girls played with dolls and doll houses, and started to develop nurturing attitudes. This gender differentiation continued throughout childhood. Boys were allowed to climb trees, roam through the woods in little packs, and come into the house covered head to toe with dirt—things that girls were not usually allowed to do. On the other hand, boys were not usually asked to mind their younger siblings, nor encouraged to offer baby sitting services, nor enrolled in home economics classes. While girls visited nursing homes with their girl scout troops, boys shivered in the forests, rubbing sticks together to start a fire. (Levant, 1992, p. 388)

Studies of children at play, with each other as well as with their parents, indicate how some observed gender differences emerge. Young boys typically play structured, rule-guided games that emphasize teamwork and competition, whereas young girls tend to play with one other girl, with whom they share personal secrets, thereby developing skills in empathy, emotional self-awareness, and emotional expression (Levant, 1992; Lever, 1976; Maccoby, 1990). From quite early ages, boys are encouraged to engage in more rough and tumble play than females (Boulton, 1994). Adults play in different ways with babies they think are of one gender or another (Frisch, 1977; Sidorowicz & Lunney, 1980). For example, adults encourage a baby they believe to be a girl to engage in more "nurturance play" with dolls and puppets, than if they think the baby is a boy (Frisch, 1977). In studies of parents interacting with their own children, Fagot (1978) observed differential treatment of boys and girls in many gender-stereotyped behaviors, most notably in help-seeking and physical closeness. In teaching situations, a quick response to a girl's request for help is likely, whereas parents often ignore or actively reject similar requests from boys (Rothbart & Rothbart, 1976). The help that is offered to boys centers on the task-oriented, with a greater emphasis on mastery and with higher standards of performance than for girls. A teaching situation with a girl is often an opportunity to cement a positive (but dependent) interpersonal relationship, however. Parents will digress from a task-oriented agenda to joke and play with a daughter more often than they will with a son (Berk, 1989). Differential interactions of parents and other adults with boys and girls, accentuating emotional nurturance styles in girls and emotionless, mastery styles in boys, continue throughout childhood and adolescence (Berk, 1989). Styles of discipline seem different for boys and girls. In at least one study, males were found to be punished with harsher physical sanctions than females (Eron & Huesmann, 1989). Male socialization to the normalcy of the anger response has roots in infancy. Adults tend to identify the crying of a child they believe to be a boy as anger, whereas they attribute equal displays of distress to fear if they think the child is a girl (Condry & Condry, 1976).

On the level of interpersonal communication, Tannen (1991) has demonstrated that boys and men tend to avoid eye contact when they talk, whereas girls and women, from the earliest stages of social development through old age, tend to face each other and look into one another's eyes. In a comprehensive review of the literature, Osborne (1991) concludes that men tend to be less empathic and less emotionally expressive than women. A number of studies show that women are more concerned than men with establishing intimate relationships and are better at doing so, both in terms of the frequency of intimate relationships and the degree of intimacy experienced in those relationships (Fischer, 1981; McAdams, 1988; Reis, 1986; Wong & Csikszentmihalyi, 1991).

These investigations and others (e.g., Belenky, Clinchy, Goldberger, & Tarule, 1986; Miller, 1986) support a gender distinction in self-esteem, recently investigated by Joseph, Markus, and Tafarodi (1992). In a series of studies, these authors indicate that self-esteem springs from different sources in men and women. The self-esteem of men can be linked to an individuation process emphasizing personal achievements. In contrast, the self-esteem of women relates to interpersonal connections and attachments to important others. A final study in this three-study series linked defensive compensatory behavior with specific violations of gender-appropriate tasks. Men with high self-esteem became defensive when they failed at independent thinking, whereas women with high self-esteem became defensive when they failed at interdependent thinking.

It would seem, then, that men in general are neither as concerned with, nor as skilled at, maintaining attachment relationships and, in fact, relate higher levels of self-esteem to independence; women, however, attribute a higher value to attachment relationships, develop more skill in them, and associate participation in them with higher levels of self-esteem.

AFFECT REGULATION

The ability to feel in control of one's life depends on the ability to regulate powerful negative feelings, particularly those related to attachment: guilt, shame, and abandonment or engulfment anxiety. Because it is used to prevent or mitigate the experience of painful attachment affect, anger is a key indicator of poor affect regulation. The more sensitive to attachment insult, that is, the less tolerant of guilt, shame, and abandonment or engulfment anxiety, the greater the anger. Given the abundance of guilt, shame, and abandonment or engulfment anxiety experienced by those afflicted with attachment deficits, we should expect that attachment abusers will present with greater levels of anger than nonabusers. Research has amply supported this proposition.

Studies with measures of anger and hostility show abusers to have elevated levels of each. This, in concert with impulsive violent behavior, indicates poor anger-management skills (Barnett & Hamberger, 1992; Barnett & Planeuax, 1989; Cahn, 1988; Dutton, 1994a; Dutton, Saunders, Starzomski, & Bartholomew, 1994; Dutton & Browning, 1988; Garcia & Kosberg, 1992; Maiuro, Cahn, & Vitaliano, 1986; Maiuro et al., 1988; Margolin, John, & Gleberman, 1988). Anger-reactivity in abusers can be seen as a result of their troubled childhoods, in light of evidence suggesting that the more anger a person is raised with, the more physiologically reactive to anger that person is liable to be (Ballard, 1992).

The immediacy with which abusers convert vulnerable feelings into anger has been described by several researchers (e.g., Dutton, Saunders, Starzomski, & Bartholomew, 1994; Ganley & Harris, 1978; Retzinger, 1991a). A series of studies using intensive video-analysis of dialogue between spouses in active verbal conflict demonstrates that the experience of shame, caused by perceived assault on the attachment bond, stimulates anger and rage (Retzinger, 1991a, 1991b; Scheff, 1990). These studies reinforce observations of clinicians who regularly report that abusers convert feelings of vulnerability into anger and rage, blaming their shame and vulnerability on their attachment figures, against whose perceived assaults they feel compelled to defend themselves (Bowlby, 1984; Gondolf, 1985; Lansky, 1987; Stosny, 1992). Anger used in this way—as a mechanism of externalization—serves an important *protective* function, guarding an already bruised or damaged or defective self from further assault of guilt, shame, and abandonment/engulfment anxiety. It also makes it possible to compensate for the internal state of powerlessness over vulnerable feelings through the exertion of power over others.

The following lines of research support the function of anger as a mechanism to externalize negative affect. The works of Epstein (1979) and Averill (1982) suggest that anger is essentially an attribution of blame. Indeed, blame distinguishes a response of anger from one of distress or upset. For example, the 3-year-old child of a client broke a valuable music box. The client's first reaction was anger as he blamed the child for his own experience of loss. He remembered his treatment, but at first only enough to replace anger for the child with self-anger, as he blamed himself for not removing the music box from the child's reach. Finally, he remembered the most crucial part of this treatment, that the accident, though distressing, did not *require* blame. At that point, the anger disappeared. He was able to comfort himself for the loss of the music box and comfort the child who felt terrible about the accident. Compassion relieved his pain and empowered him as well as the child. In contrast, to sustain the pain-relief and energy-surge of *anger*, one must *look* for reasons to blame.

The causal relationship of negative affect to anger and aggression has been established in a series of experiments by a number of researchers, reviewed by Berkowitz (1990). The neoassocionistic theory of emotions put forth by Berkowitz (1990) identifies a complex network of associations of bad feelings that can produce anger arousal without conscious awareness. The rapidity of these connections, measured in milliseconds, far outruns the ability to translate them into words. Thus, many of the associations never develop what Berkowitz refers to as higher cognitive processes to regulate them. This research supports the conventional wisdom that anger comes most easily when we're already feeling depressed, anxious, tense, or just plain bad. Thus anger protects the already aroused or injured self from further harm. Carol Tavris (1987) combines her version of the neo-associonistic view with an explicit depiction of anger as externalizer of vulnerable feelings. She points out that Freud had it backwards in his famous description of depression as anger turned inward. Now the evidence suggests that anger is depression turned outward.

Anger as a reaction to perceived threats to self-esteem has been established in the work of da Gloria (1984), Feshbach (1970), Kernis, Grannemann, and Barclay (1989), Novaco (1975), Rosenzweig (1944), Rule and Nesdale (1974), Wills (1981), and Zillman (1978). This function of anger is especially important in attachment relationships. Personal well-being is so dependent on the ability to negotiate attachment relationships that virtually every dispute with attachment figures in some sense puts the self at stake. Here anger protects the self by blaming attachment difficulties on abused partners.

The complex role of anger in seizing power—by energizing behavior, advertising potency and determination, and by overriding feelings of anxiety, vulnerability, and ego threat—is reviewed by Novaco (1975). This line of evidence suggests that anger is the temporary elixir of self-ache. During anger arousal, cracks and holes within the self seem suddenly filled. Doubt temporarily gives way to the artificial certainty that comes from failure to see all but one narrow perspective. Because it is meant to mobilize the organism for action, it "protects" the individual from action-inhibiting doubt.

The stimulation of anger and aggression to protect the self from the painful assault of shame has been explored by Katz (1988), Lansky (1987), Lewis (1971, 1976, 1989), Retzinger (1991a), Scheff (1989, 1990), and Tangney (1991; Tangney, Wagner, Fletcher, & Gramzow, 1992). It may be that all anger not stimulated by physical pain blazes on the fuel of shame. The biosocial function of shame, to renew a damaged or suspended attachment bond, only reinforces the connection to anger, if abusers suffer the compulsion to blame their shame on attachment figures.

A survey of college students (Harris, 1992) indicates that males, particularly those who had behaved aggressively in the past, were significantly more likely to believe that aggressive behavior would reduce their anger-reactivity and elevate their moods. The stimulant effects of anger may work on anxiety and agitation like Ritalin(TM) works on hyperactivity in children. A modicum of empirical support for this contention comes from a recent study by Jacobson and Gottman (1993), which shows that the heart rates of the most violent spouse abusers, whom the authors call, "vagal reactors," *decrease* during abusive exchange. It's a pity this important study did not include brain wave measurements. These might have revealed that vagal reactors use anger to replace theta with beta waves, establishing a connection with attention deficit hyperactivity disorder (ADHD). The subsequently increased concentration allowed vagal reactors to pursue what was probably the overriding meaning of their lives: seeking a kind of moral validation by paying back those they perceive as persecutors.

ANGER AND MORAL IMPERATIVE

This notion of anger as an affect-externalization mechanism is very different from the myth of uncontrollable anger leading to aggression. The special deficit of the attachment abuser has little to do with controlling anger and everything to do with regulating the guilt, shame, and abandonment or engulfment anxiety they convert into anger. The real problem is their dichotomous emotional world, which allows them to feel hardly anything but powerless vulnerability on the one hand, and temporarily empowering anger on the other. Anger externalizes the feeling of powerlessness, making possible the illusion that it can be relieved through the exertion of power over others. The more anger is directed at loved ones, the more guilt, shame, and abandonment or engulfment anxiety it provokes, stimulating still more anger.

Yet the trigger for abusive behavior is not an uncontrollable accumulation of anger. The actual link to aggression is the almost moral imperative abusers give to their "right," if not "duty," to restore personal power, albeit through the distorted and illusory means of exerting power over loved ones. Some authors argue that this sort of moral imperative is at the heart of all criminal aggression (e.g., Katz, 1988). I believe it explains the link between anger and aggression against loved ones. For those whose lives are riddled with the chaos of unregulated guilt, shame, and abandonment or engulfment anxiety, anger provides an artificial focus and moral certainty, which abusive behavior seems to *validate*.

Figure 4.1 suggests how anger externalizes the sense of powerlessness created by the experience of guilt, shame, and abandonment or engulfment anxiety, making possible the illusion, driven by a kind of moral imperative, that personal power can, and *should*, be restored by exerting power over

Figure 4.1 Anger as affect externalizer.

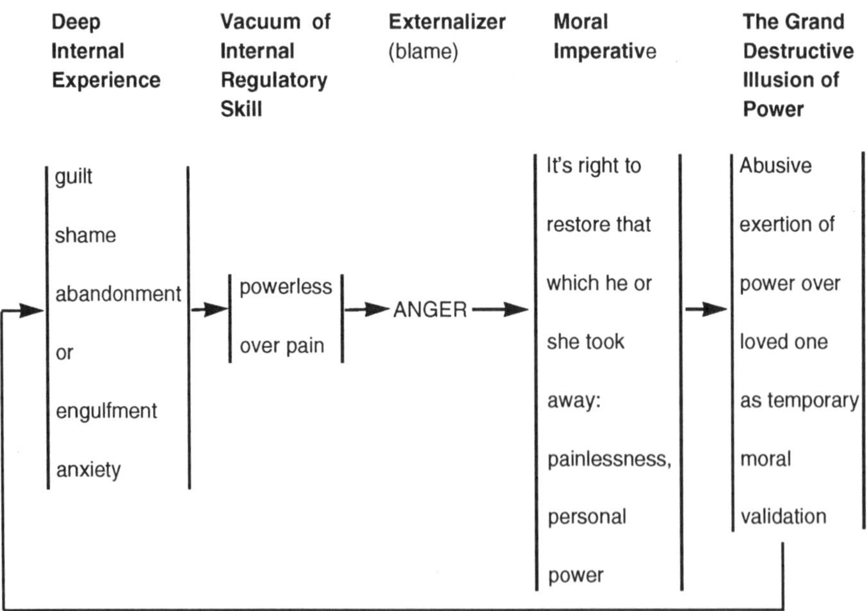

Table 4.1 Anger Arousal Cycle

Physiological	*Cognitive*	*Behavior*	*Psychological*
"Fight or flight" instinct of *all* mammals enhanced by hurt and fear surge of energy pain-numbing goes to all muscle groups and all organs	Rigid, narrow range of thoughts Impaired: • encoding • recall • performance-competence • interpretation • social cue utilization	*Ward-off* perceived attacker by attempting to: • control/neutralize • warn • threaten • intimidate • injure (feelings and/or body)	*Avoid feeling:* disregarded unimportant accused devalued rejected *powerless* *unlovable* *unfit for human contact* An *anger junkie* uses anger for: • energy/motivation • pain-relief • confidence • enhanced sense of self • avoiding depressed mood

those perceived to have created the internal sense of powerlessness.

This interplay of a sense of moral justification, with the compulsion to externalize the intolerable feeling of pain and powerlessness as the fault of the attachment figure, is why, as Jacobson and Gottman point out (1993), anger management programs for abusers miss the point. Abusers hear wonderful advice like, "It's okay to be angry, just don't hurt anyone with it," as, "You deserve to feel powerless and morally impotent." Treatment must provide attachment abusers with alternative means to validate and process vulnerable feelings in ways that restore a powerful internal sense of self. At the same time, they must provide a nonshaming interpersonal morality to diminish the external chaos perceived by the abuser.

Once again, either extreme of the self-organizational continuum (diffuse on the one hand or narrow and rigid on the other) will fall susceptible to the use of anger as protection from internal and interpersonal chaos.

We can better understand how and why abusers use anger for affect externalization and (temporary) moral certainty by understanding how the anger-arousal cycle works physiologically, cognitively, behaviorally, and psychologically, as depicted in Table 4.1.

THE ANGER-AROUSAL CYCLE

Physiological Component

Anger mobilizes the organism for action (Izard & Schwartz, 1986). As part of the fight or flight instinct we share with all mammals, anger is the most powerful of human experience in terms of energy utilization. Anger is the only emotion that activates every organ and muscle group of the body. The biochemicals secreted in the brain in the experience of intense emotion—most notably the hormone epinephrine and the neurotransmitter norepinephrine, and their various neural precursors—are experienced much like an amphetamine and analgesic. The experience of *anger numbs pain and provides a surge of energy.* To produce a state of anger arousal, the sympathetic nervous system activates, heart rate increases (unless already elevated, in which case it may decrease, as happens with many stimulants), blood pressure elevates, eyes dilate, digestion halts, messages of physical pain transmitted by nerve endings are blocked, and a surge of energy is produced—all necessary physiological responses for flight or fight, all necessary to serve the primary function of anger as protection of the organism from external attack.

Cognitive Component

Heightened emotional arousal in general has disruptive effects on cognitive processes (Eysenck, 1982). Negative affective states produce a narrowing of focus and attention (Broadbent, 1971; Eysenck, 1976) and a reduction in the range of cue utilization (Easterbrook 1959), or a kind of cognitive contraction. Experimental data suggest that cognitive functions particularly distorted and biased by anger-arousal include encoding (Dodge & Newman, 1981; Dodge & Tomlin, 1987), interpretation (Dodge & Coie, 1987; Dodge & Frame, 1982; Dodge, Pettit, McClaskey, & Brown, 1986; Slaby & Guerra, 1988; Waas, 1988), and performance competence (Dodge et al., 1986). These studies confirm the old saw about being so mad you can't think straight. The diminished capacity for judgment allows the angry person to see only justification for anger, if not aggression.

Cue utilization is especially problematic when the angry person misinterprets the response of attachment figures, and then, through the emotional inter-regulation mechanism of attachment relationships, stimulates the actual anger in loved ones he had incorrectly attributed to them.

Behavioral Component

The goal of the action impulse (that which, uninhibited, leads to overt behavior) of the anger-arousal cycle is to ward-off the perceived potential attacker with aggressive behavior (Berkowitz, 1990; Berkowitz & Heimer, 1989). This may be accomplished with attempts to control–neutralize, warn–threaten, intimidate, or inflict injury on the feelings or body of another.

Psychological Component

In an environment in which humankind has long since prevailed over the saber-toothed tiger, wooly mammoth, and other nightmarish predators, the principal function of anger is to protect us from psychic pain. An arousal sysztem meant for short bursts of ferocious energy is now evoked for prolonged, if not continual, bouts with noxious stimuli in daily interactions. The physiological strains of the anger-arousal cycle (see Table 4.1) are, in prolonged activation, sources of daily stress-reactions, with serious consequences for emotional and physical health (Diamond, 1982; Greer & Morris, 1975; Novaco, 1975; Storr, 1988; Williams et al., 1980; Williams & Williams, 1993).

The crucial question for treatment concerns the nature of the psychic pain temporarily relieved by anger in attachment relationships. The following list of items was compiled from responses of more than 300 abusers in treatment who were asked to note which feelings made them the angriest at their loved ones (Stosny, 1992):

- disregarded
- unimportant
- accused, especially if falsely or inaccurately
- devalued
- rejected
- powerless, like a child
- unlovable
- unfit for human contact.

First, the reader is cautioned against regarding this list as independently collected data. It was compiled in the process of a treatment technique to teach abusers to put emotional experience into words, for the purpose of establishing constructive skill to regulate them. In response to "What makes you the maddest at home?," group members called out nominees for the list, which were written on a blackboard by the group leader. Most often the items nominated for the list were behaviors, with the corresponding feelings suggested by the group leader. Even though an item made the final list only with the general affirmation of group members, an obvious therapeutic purpose, antithetical to nonbiased, independent data-gathering, dominated the process.

But although the list cannot be regarded as data, it provides a useful tool in understanding what kind of circumstances contribute to activation of the anger-arousal cycle in attachment relationships. Not only do the items on the list represent responses to perceived assaults on the sense of self and to self-esteem, they are reactions to perceived attacks on the attachment bond. They represent, arguably, an array of the most severe, nontraumatic psychic pain. They are various nuances of shame, a withdraw-hide emotion, experienced as a sinking feeling and a depletion of energy (Tomkins, 1963, 1991). Anger provides an immediate surge of energy and blurring of pain—a feeling of power—to replace the powerlessness of shame.

> Anger not only increases tension and impulsiveness, it is associated with an elevated sense of self-assurance. The increased energy and self-assurance can facilitate constructive action that ameliorates depression. (Izard & Schwartz, 1986, p. 64)

The cognitive rigidity experienced during anger arousal replaces the thought diffusion and general mental confusion experienced in shame, as the attachment figure becomes, for a moment, nothing other than a perceived attacker.

So the abuser uses anger for energy and motivation, pain-relief, certainty, confidence (a more powerful if transitory sense of self), as a means to militate out of depressed mood, and as a means of moral validation. (Note that none of these uses of anger requires explosive rage, which would ruin its intended function and, therefore, would have never been reinforced.) In a mundane sense, most of us occasionally use anger for these functions. For instance, we employ anger for energy and motivation to do tasks we really do not want to perform, like staying up all night to fill out income tax forms. Anger at the self, for having procrastinated to the last minute, and anger at the government, for creating such complex tax requirements, provide the energy to do the exceedingly unpleasant work. We may sometimes use a form of anger—grumpiness—to allay social anxiety. (This is often seen at parties in which some people are overly critical of everything, at least until they warm up, i.e., until their social anxiety is allayed, and the analgesic effects of anger made unnecessary.) One can usually tell which academic papers were written in anger, when the polarizing cognitive effect of anger in response to previous criticism compels authors to staunchly defend positions of which they have no genuine conviction. Perhaps most often we use anger to keep from feeling hurt and rejected when insulted or accused.

Attachment abusers use anger for the above purposes more than nonabusers. They form habits in their use, a kind of neural-familiarity (a recurring sequence of neural firing) that has the outward manifestations of addictive behavior. A great many abusers are addicted to the chemical ride—the amphetamine and analgesic experience—of anger; they are anger-junkies, who will go to any length and stretch for any justification for a jolt of anger to lift them to levels of energy that, for some depressed abusers merely match what is normal for most of us, and, for some of the distracted and anxious, merely direct concentration and purpose.

INTERACTION OF DEFICITS IN ATTACHMENT AND AFFECT REGULATION

An interaction between deficits in attachment and affect regulation explains the high recidivist rate of attachment abuse: The less skill in affect management, the more damage done to attachment relationships by blaming attachment figures for the abuser's negative affect (for "making me feel bad"). His retaliatory assault on the very attachment bond he desperately needs creates more shame, guilt, and abandonment anxiety to mismanage.

An Emotional Learning Disability

A useful metaphor for understanding the abuser's processing of affective information is that of "emotional learning disability." Abusers never learned mature ways of processing powerful affective information. They react to hurt and disappointment much like a child in a temper tantrum. (If you hurt the feelings of a two year-old he'll hit you.) Anger functions as his primary pain-reliever, just as the mature responses of self-validation, self-soothing, compassion for self and others, and the honest expression of hurt or shame, are pain-relievers for adults unafflicted by the emotional learning disability.[1]

The implications for treatment of abusers seem enormous. With their noted dependency needs (which they loathe) and low level of skill in negotiating attachment relationships, abusers know neither how to behave nor feel in the intimate relationships for which they have intense need. With poor internal regulation of their experience, they vacillate between fear of engulfment and fear of abandonment. Their attachment deficits create continual anxiety, perceived rejection, shame, and guilt, which they have little skill to regulate.

The concept of attachment abuse predicts that a class of people with attachment deficits, underscored through normative socialization and interacting with deficits in affect-regulation, will be disproportionally represented among attachment abusers. Thus the concept of attachment abuse predicts that the most violent people in intimate relationships will be young children and young men, a prediction supported by the available data (Archer, 1994; Bureau of Justice Statistics, 1988; Gelles & Cornell, 1990; Stark & Flitcraft, 1985; Straus & Gelles, 1988).

---

[1] One need not necessarily rely on this concept as a metaphor. The notion of mature versus immature emotional processing is similar to Vaillant's concept of mature versus immature defense mechanisms (1977). Another way of testing propositions derived from the concept is to measure the amount of anger used as affect-management, as suggested in Chapter Seven. The hypotheses would be that abusers will have immature defense mechanisms and elevated levels of anger directly related to general vulnerability, including shame.

CHAPTER SUMMARY

The literature of empirical research and clinical anecdote describes abusers as hurt individuals with grave attachment needs and little skill in negotiating attachment relationships. They suffer internal power-voids, sustained by a poor sense of self and interacting deficiencies in attachment skills and affect regulation. They have no way of easing their hurt except to blame it on the people closest to them. They use anger to numb pain and to seize power outside themselves, in the vain hope of filling the inner void through a distorted sort of moral self-justification.

5 A New Response for Clinicians in the Prevention of Emotional Abuse and Violence

A treatment approach emphasizing attachment dysfunction features a unique advantage in the movement to prevent emotional abuse and violence within families. Coincidentally, this advantage affords individual clinicians the opportunity to expand and deepen levels of practice to include community outreach and consultation services. More important, it offers hope that we will not exacerbate *hidden abuse* of and by our clients. This chapter describes how to fulfill these hopes, with a warning of what often happens when we fail to detect hidden abuse. First, the bad news.

CONVENTIONAL TREATMENT EXACERBATES ATTACHMENT ABUSE

The beginning phases of conventional family, couples, and individual treatment exposes problem areas for work in the course of the therapy. The predominant affective range of clients at this point of treatment usually includes heightened anxiety, guilt, and shame. Although an initial response of negative emotion can be of benefit to the therapeutic process, it creates havoc with attachment abusers who lack the skill to regulate powerful negative affect. Professional helpers must not underestimate the *danger of doing conventional treatment of attachment abusers before they learn emo-*

tional-regulation skills. I have met many scores of clients who suffered increased abuse after a few sessions of conventional treatment at individual, couples, and family levels. The most common case is the abusive couple who, even when controlled in the company of the therapist, fights ferociously after the session. In fact, a subdued reaction by couples in the therapy may indicate a submerged iceberg of shame that, in private, explodes in anger and aggression.

A particularly tragic, but not unusual, example occurred when a well-meaning psychiatrist intervened in a family that had no history of physical abuse. Ostensibly, the family came to therapy for help with their teenage son. An obvious triangulation was in place in which the mother continually countermanded the father's efforts to discipline the son, even when the couple had agreed privately on appropriate sanctions. Failing to interpret the conspicuousness of the triangle as one piece of clinical evidence of hidden attachment abuse, the psychiatrist elicited a promise from the mother to break up the triangle. Of course, in a family whose members possess some degree of emotional regulatory skill, this would have been sound intervention. But in a family afflicted with attachment abuse, it was disastrous. Unbeknownst to the psychiatrist, the father had ridiculed and put the boy down continually for the past 15 years. Now feeling abandoned by his lifelong protector, the adolescent's disrespectful behavior toward his father escalated. The two began to goad one another. The boy's face, according to the parents, would glow with rage. The father, in short order, reacted to this intensified defiance with violence. The boy fought back, was overpowered, suffered a broken jaw. Battered and humiliated, he slashed his wrists just after the hysterical mother called the police.

Without assessing the potential for attachment abuse, even individual therapy can be dangerous. One case involved a man whose treatment included reconstructing memories of childhood abuse. Numbed from 2 years of emotional degradation that had been undisclosed to the therapist, the wife could not react to this newly excavated information with sufficient sympathy to suit her needy husband. His unregulated shame once again turned to fury and aggression. She was hospitalized for several days with a fractured ear drum, two broken ribs, and a dislocated shoulder.

A therapist treating a passive-aggressive woman privately made great progress toward developing the client's assertiveness skills. Though informed of emotional abuse in the family, the therapist must have been unaware of the propensity for attachment abuse to move upwards on its continuum of destruction. Predictably, the untreated husband felt overwhelmed with abandonment-anxiety sparked by his wife's emerging assertiveness. This was a particularly sad story because the woman told me that she thoroughly liked her therapist and didn't want to make *her* feel bad by keeping appointments with bruises and black eyes. So she frequently missed appointments, only to be questioned about her resistance to treatment.

Another therapist challenged a woman whose self-esteem had been eroded by a decade of subtle emotional abuse. "If you're such a good mother," he chided, "why are your children so angry?" If the therapist had asked this question of himself, he might have figured out that the children were angry because the household was abusive, as even a cursory familiarity with the literature on anger in children would have informed him. *When children are symptomatic, particularly angry and anxious, attachment abuse is always a clear possibility.* This is not to say that self-defeating parental practices are not an important problem in attachment abuse cases. It is to say that the abuse must be stopped and emotional regulation techniques learned before commencing treatment of dysfunctional styles of interacting among family members.

A dangerous myth among some clinicians is that abusers exhibit explosive anger. In reality, many fear their anger and are especially afraid to show it outside the home, including to therapists who must inform them of the confidentiality exception for cases involving child abuse. It may be that the majority of abusers present as inhibited in the expression of anger. They will almost invariably present themselves as victims. The all too frequent misinterpretation of these signs by therapists causes incalculable suffering when it takes the form of interventions to force "over-controlled" persons to "get in touch with their anger." Never mind that this notion of treatment is a relic of the past, pretty well debunked by evidence showing that it actually teaches people to be more angry and aggressive (Biaggio, 1987; Lewis & Bucher, 1992; Tavris, 1987); urging attachment abusers to experience more anger has disastrous consequences for them and their loved ones. A review of the literature on anger arousal cited in the previous chapter indicates that anger most often serves as a generalized response to dysphoria, particularly physical discomfort, disappointment, sadness, loss, grief, guilt, fear of abandonment, engulfment anxiety, and shame. When clients funnel the experience of these complex emotional phenomena into the generalized container of anger, they subvert their ability to understand and regulate their true experience, intensify their proclivity to blame and to avoid personal responsibility for their internal experience (i.e., externalize their locus of control), engage in a relentless anger/depression roller-coaster ride that requires increased anger (as they become tolerant of, and dependent on, the biochemical substrata of anger arousal) to militate out of depressed mood. As it obscures the deeper and more complex experiences that cause it, a frequent response of anger further alienates clients from their core selves. And, of course, social havoc befalls those with already poor interpersonal skills or deficient social cue utilization, which anger arousal further distort. However, it is abundantly easy to get hurt people to feel angry. Any incompetent therapist can do it.

One therapist told an abuser that, due to his "suppression and stubborn denial," he had "pools of anger all over his body" that had to be "let out." Once again, this a metaphor from the dark ages of psychology, having the same validity as the claim that one has "tiny erections" all over the body because one has suppressed or denied sexual feelings. We know that anger occurs in arousal cycles with measurable baseline, peak, and post arousal dimensions. It cannot be "stored all over the body," although the constructive mediators of anger, such as blame, internal powerlessness, and general cynicism, may constitute trait-like mind-sets that produce frequent cycles of anger arousal. Of course, these cannot be "gotten out" and will only be reinforced by therapists urging clients to experience more overt anger. Constructive mediators must be changed by altering the meaning-making process of which they are part. In any event, this particular client, like many so instructed by therapists unaware that they were treating attachment abusers, "let out his pools of anger" all over the head and body of his "disrespectful" teenage daughter.

A colleague in charge of the inpatient treatment of child sexual abusers compared their "over-controlled" experience of anger to "emotional anorexia," whereas violent abusers, he theorized, had "emotional bulimia" in the expression of anger. The confusion of anger with food is a philosophical quandary unto itself. Clinically, it creates an atmosphere about which releasees of the institution candidly joke that all they had to do to get out of the hospital (and have access to more children) was "get in touch with their anger." Their ample anger at the hospital staff, deliberately recalled at the time of prerelease plethysmography, helped them to pass the test with no sign of arousal. (Obviously they were aware that resentment is a powerful dampener of sexual arousal, Masters, 1993). The free and frequent expression of anger was taken by the hospital staff as a sign that patients were no longer "in denial," which apparently, in their way of thinking, inidicated successful treatment. The practice of releasing child molesters when levels of overt anger have risen above those at admission is especially disturbing in light of suggestive findings that level of anger seems to distinguish child molesters from rapists (e.g., Marhsall, Laws, & Barbaree, 1990).

The horror stories of conventional treatment aggravating abuse can go on for volumes. Of the 600 clients we have treated, nearly one third—virtually all who had been in prior treatment—suffered increased levels of abuse following each therapy session that did not address deficits in affect regulation and attachment skills. Rarely did these people continue in their prior treatment for more than a few sessions; their therapists probably never learned of the abuse that had occurred prior to treatment nor of that which happened during the treatment.

GUIDE FOR DETECTING HIDDEN ATTACHMENT ABUSE

Generally, there are two types of hidden attachment abuse. In the first, the principals honestly don't realize that they behave abusively. This can be the case even in the presence of serious violence, for such people have no idea of what normal family functioning might be like. However, in the more common instance of hidden abuse, the parties know quite well that emotional or physical abuse takes place but, due to shame or naivete, dismiss it as a symptom of some other problem (usually "communication,") which they prefer to talk about in therapy. Clinicians must take great care not to commit the same tragic error as their clients by ignoring the possibility of covert attachment abuse. The damage of attachment abuse will only worsen in the throes of emotionally charged content raised by conventional treatment that tacitly presumes a modicum of skill in affect regulation.

In every manner of practice, clinicians should add the following safeguards to their treatment protocols: (1) Screen all clients for the possibility of hidden attachment abuse. (2) Don't attempt conventional therapy until emotional regulation skills are developed. (3) Secure a contract in which clients agree to avoid discussing hot issues until they have learned emotional regulation techniques. (4) Follow-up with drop-outs. (5) Administer the Conflict Tactics Scale (Straus, 1979) to treatment completers at least quarterly for the first year following treatment.

The Conflict Tactics Scale (CTS) should be part of intake forms, along with a symptom questionnaire to assess anxiety, anger, and hostility. The CTS measures the amount of verbal aggression and physical abuse that has taken place in the past year and is applicable to all attachment relationships. (Try giving it to a few ongoing clients of whom you never suspected abuse; you may be quite surprised!) But even on the CTS, shame-ridden abusers and victims tend to minimize—and outright lie—about the degree and severity of abuse (e.g., Tolman & Bennett, 1990). Clinicians must be armed with additional techniques to detect abuse in its most concealed forms. Danger signs that signal a high risk of hidden attachment abuse include sometimes subtle *deficits* in:

1. perspective-taking,
2. sympathy for self and loved ones,
3. validation of the emotional experience of self and loved ones,
4. emotional vocabulary.

A reliable assessment question for deficit number one asks the client to assume the perspective of the attachment figure with whom he or she describes conflict. Most clients will have trouble with this on the first try or two, depending on the level of current affect-arousal. The red flag emerges when repeated attempts to get the client to take the perspective of attachment figures utterly fail. However, don't give up too soon, particularly if the client is unaware of core vulnerable feelings. Here's how it often goes:

Client: "She gets me so pissed."
Therapist: "Why do you think she does that?"
Client: "She's trying to get me mad."
Therapist: "But why would she want to do that?"
Client: "She's trying to hurt me."
Therapist: "Why?"
Client: "Cause that's the way she is!"
Therapist: "Why is she like that about this particular thing?" (pause)
Client: "I guess because she's hurt."

With this admission, the client abruptly changes his construction of meaning. The therapist might draw the client's attention to the physiological signs of dissipating anger or anxiety: muscles relax, face returns to normal color, countenance and voice soften. As a precursor to treatment, the therapist might ask at this point whether the client feels better with his compassionate response. This good feeling becomes the internal reward and motivation to use compassion as an incompatible response to anger arousal.

Of course, an obvious indicator of deficit number one is a totally unrealistic perspective, such as, an infant "defies me just to hurt my feelings."

Use of the Attachment Compassion Scale (see Appendix B) can be of enormous help for estimating the ability of clients to regulate their own anger by taking the point of view of attachment figures. It, too, can be adapted for all attachment relationships.

Deficit number two, lack of sympathy for self and loved ones, is assessed by the client's emotional tone describing himself or while taking the perspective of loved ones. If it includes contempt or derision, or if intensity increases rather than decreases, a red flag flies.

Assessment of deficit number three, the ability to validate the emotional experience of self and loved ones, centers first on whether the client's own emotional experience is affirmed, "I feel hurt by what she said," or *invalidated*, "It doesn't bother me, I just want her to stop it," or, "It's stupid to be feeling like this." Assessing the ability to validate the emotional experience of loved ones turns on whether the emotional experience of the attachment figure is affirmed, "I see how he feels that way," or, "She's wrong, but I understand how she feels that way," or *invalidated*, "He doesn't have any right to feel that way," or, "How dare her think like that!" Note that this applies not to the behavior of attachment figures but to their internal emotional reality. For example, "I know that he feels hurt, and I'm sorry about that, but he had no right to say those hurtful things to me. It just makes it worse for both of us." This actually represents an advanced level of compassion, in which one understands and validates the hurt that causes abusive behavior, while holding firmly to the fact that abusive behavior is intolerable, as much for the harm it does to the perpetrator as to the victim.

Deficit number four, lack of emotional vocabulary, creates a high risk of converting vulnerable feelings into anger and aggression. If clients are unable to identify which feelings give rise to their anger, anxiety, or obsessions, they probably have little way of coping with those vulnerable feelings other than converting them into anger. The ability to label emotional experience is the first step in processing that information in new, constructive ways.

If any of the above deficits are found to exist, clinicians should do at least a modified version of the Compassion Workshop. Secure agreements from clients not to discuss hot issues with attachment figures before emotional regulatory skills develop. This takes about 3 weeks of practicing the emotional regulation techniques of the Compassion Workshop, based on self-compassion and compassion for loved ones (see Chapter 7).

Follow-up contact with treatment completers is a necessity in this high-risk population. We administer the CTS to victims by phone quarterly, and give them open permission to contact us as soon as relapse seems a possibility.

Once again, for the safety of your clients, *(1) Screen everyone for the possibility of hidden attachment abuse. (2) Don't attempt conventional therapy until emotional regulation techniques are learned. (3) Secure a contract in which clients agree to avoid discussing hot issues until they have learned emotional regulation techniques. (4) Follow-up with drop-outs. (5) Administer the CTS to treatment completers quarterly for the first year following treatment.*

Diagnosis and testing often tell you that you have a victim in treatment, but not the abuser. In that case, the first thing to do is take appropriate safety precautions. This means notifying child and adult protective services when physical abuse is present or imminent. If the victim is an adult, strongly emphasize the importance to everyone in the family that the abuser get treatment. If the victim is a parent, an especially helpful handout is, "What Abuse Can Do to You and Your Family" (Figure 5.1).

Figure 5.1 What abuse can do to you and your family.

- All *victims* of family abuse, all *abusers,* and all *children* of victims lose some degree of dignity and autonomy.
- At least half suffer from clinical anxiety and/or depression.
- Most lack self-esteem.
- Witnessing abuse makes a child 10 times more likely to become either an abuser or a victim of abuse. As adults they are at increased risk of alcoholism, drug abuse, criminality, mental health problems, and poverty.
- Symptoms of children in abusive families may include one or more of the following:

  depression, anxiety, school problems, aggressiveness, hyperactivity, low self-esteem, exhibiting over-emotionality (weepiness, anger, excitability) or no emotions at all.
- Emotional abuse is often more psychologically damaging than physical abuse.
- Abuse almost always gets worse without intervention.
- Symptoms of victims often include one or more of the following:

  trouble sleeping (can't get to sleep or wake up in the middle of the night)
  frequent periods of sadness and crying
  continual worry and anxiety
  obsessions
  excessive anger
  confusion/impaired decision-making
  low self-esteem.
- Key questions to answer from deep within your heart:

  Do I like myself?
  Am I able to realize my personal potential?
  Am I treated with dignity and respect?
  Do I feel safe?
  Do my children like themselves?
  Are they able to realize their fullest potential?

Most of the material in the Compassion Workshop is generic in design, to fill deficits in attachment skills and affect regulation, and is, therefore, quite useful to victims. I have found that an important empowerment element for victims seeking treatment on their own is to expose them to much of the same material as the abusers get. This has two positive effects. In the first place, victims see that the problem is clearly within the abuser and that nothing they say or do justifies abuse. This goes a long way toward relieving victim guilt. Second, it shows that the abuser has a treatable condition and that the only hope of maintaining an attachment relationship with him or her lies in treatment. Roughly 70% of the victims who begin the Compassion Workshop on their own are able to get their abusers into treatment, by taking a compassionate, tough-love stand. Of those who do not, virtually all of them are empowered to leave the abusive relationship.

EXPANDING PRACTICE WHILE PREVENTING ABUSE

As the first line of help that many victims and their abusers seek, mental health clinicians can play a key role in the *prevention* of severe abuse and violence, while at the same time expanding their own practice. The key is to attract clients before abusive patterns become entrenched. To that end, the following served as a regular announcement in *The Washington Post:*

LOVE WITHOUT HURT
Brief, intensive treatment for
Conflictive, hurtful, or
Abusive relationships
Anger/Anxiety Regulation
Compassion Workshops

This announcement proved abundantly successful in attracting abusers and victims in early phases of abuse for one simple reason: It doesn't mention violence. As families proceed along the continuum of abuse, denial of its brutal ends becomes increasingly compelling. Thus the seeming extremity of the mere suggestion of violence scares off potential victims and alienates potential abusers in families not yet visited by violence.

Groups based on the Prevention Manual of the Compassion Workshop can be marketed to high schools, colleges, graduate schools, professional training programs, hospitals, residential treatment facilities, day treatment programs, 12-step and other self-help groups, managed health care organizations, churches and synagogues, corporations, prisons, correctional facilities, and nursing homes. (The Prevention Manual is available from Intermedia, 1-800-553-8336.)

COMMUNITY OUTREACH EFFORTS

The virtual absence of clinicians in community efforts to prevent family violence may in part account for the after-the-fact nature of such efforts. Most community outreach programs concentrate on preventing *further* violence in already violent homes. With a public health problem as severe as family violence (now statistically related to all major social problems), primary prevention methods are of paramount importance. Family violence prevention efforts should target previolent and preemotionally abusive behaviors before they congeal into treatment-resistant patterns. In other words, primary prevention in the community should be aimed at the very foundations of the continuum of attachment abuse (see Figure I.3, p. vi).

Because the occasional failure of compassion (that leads us to deliberately or inadvertently hurt the feelings of loved ones) is a universal phenomenon of family life, enhancement of attachment bonds through training in compassion serves as a common therapeutic goal, free of the formidable resistance endemic to conventional treatment for abusers. Due to its strategic place as the first leg on the continuum of attachment abuse, the elimination of failures of compassion prevents progression along the track of pain that results in violence.

By targeting the least severe forms of abuse in ways that engage potential abusers, outreach efforts can be directed through small community and church groups. The Prevention Manual of the Compassion Workshop (available from the author) has been adapted for such a prevention program, divided into two 4-week workshops. The first addresses the primary barrier to functional attachment interactions by teaching skills in emotional regulation. The second 4-week workshop develops attachment relationship skills, specifically mutual empowerment to avoid power struggles, closeness–distance regulation, assertiveness training, conflict resolution, and regulation of the dual terror that reeks havoc in family relationships: fear of abandonment and fear of engulfment.

Community prevention efforts should aim at families experiencing: *conflictive, hurtful, or abusive interactions.*

Initial prevention efforts should concentrate on neighborhoods of high risk, as determined by police calls for domestic violence assistance. Reduction in domestic violence calls to the police in targeted areas, along with posttest reduction of risk factors in potential abusers (verbal aggression, low self-esteem, external locus of control, propensity for power struggles, emotional dysregulation, narrow and rigid belief systems) constitute outcome indicators of program effectiveness.

There is enormous opportunity for clinicians to serve as advisors to community and church groups in prevention of family violence, in programs based on the above described adaptation of the Compassion Workshop.

CHAPTER SUMMARY

The construct of attachment abuse offers an opportunity for primary prevention of the public health problem of family violence. Coincidentally, it offers clinicians a chance to expand their practice within the community. More important, it assures us that we will not exacerbate hidden abuse through use of conventional treatment methods that are inappropriate for attachment abusers who lack skill in affect regulation.

Comprehensive screening for hidden abuse includes standardized instruments and methods of role-playing to assess the level of deficiency in compassion. Clinicians are sorely needed to serve as consultants to programs designed to prevent all forms of emotional abuse and domestic violence.

6 Compassion and Therapeutic Morality

The clinical treatment of attachment abusers raises important ethical questions, regarding how clinicians go about helping clients behave morally. The very urgency of the need to protect potential and actual victims of abuse cannot blind us to the danger of misusing our own power and authority to subvert the will of clients. We must not forget that even education is value-laden and that, when educating the vulnerable, we run the risk of using power and authority to impose the majority's familial values on a minority. For this compelling ethical reason, treatment should avoid the sometimes intense temptation to espouse particular familial values and strive, instead, for the nurturance of moral agency, that is, to help clients build the skill to make moral judgments and to act on them with integrity. Fortunately, the nurturance of moral agency is not only an ethical pursuit for clinicians, it has tremendous therapeutic value for clients.

It will be argued below that moral agency is the product of a powerful sense of self, fortified by the internal reward of compassionate constructions of self and others. Thus the subject of morality can itself be therapeutic when used overtly in treatment to enhance rather than impugn the self. The Compassion Workshop teaches attachment abusers to regulate their sense of personal well-being by doing that which helps them grow rich in the healing properties of compassionate morality. In simple behavioral terms, this constitutes an operant conditioning model, emphasizing that, as a function of the internal reward of the survival-based need to form attachment and social bonds, people like themselves more when they experience compassion than when they don't; genuine self-esteem depends on our capacity for compassionate morality. In this context, clients experience moral reasoning as therapeutic and empowering rather than a source of guilt and shame. They enjoy the hope of transcending an abusive past by growing into the genuinely powerful condition of moral agency.

REWARDS AND PUNISHMENTS OF EXTERNAL VERSUS INTERNAL MOTIVATION

Social acceptance, the reward of *external* motivation for moral behavior, seems to matter more in its loss than in its keeping. Because we seem to fear the loss of social acceptance more than we appreciate having it, fear of punishment dominates external motivation for moral behavior. Specific kinds of punishment can take the form of institutionalized sanctions (e.g., legal penalties), retaliation (a vengeful brother-in-law), social reprimands ("The neighbors will talk,") or pejorative labelling: "child abuser," "wife-beater," "granny-basher." Due to the primacy of the human propensity to avoid punishment, external motivation runs the risk of making us more sneaky and manipulative than moral, as, for example, studies of child discipline attest (e.g., Eron, Walder, Huesmann, & Lefkowitz, 1974; Redd, Morris, & Martin, 1975).

Internal motivation for prosocial behavior can be self-enhancing, as with the experience of compassion, or punitive, as in the experience of guilt, shame, and abandonment anxiety. The distinction lies in whether I feel good about myself for doing the right thing or simply do the right thing because I'll feel bad about myself if I don't. Of course, the same propensity that leads us to avoid external punishment through covert means functions internally, in the form of reality-distorting coping mechanisms to reduce guilt, shame, and abandonment anxiety, most notably denial of personal responsibility. But a more central problem with internal negative reinforcers lies in their reliance on bad feelings about the self as behavioral modifiers, the force of which necessarily decline in states of dysphoria. The person who already feels bad about himself is likely to convert the dysphoria into anger (Berkowitz, 1990), become more impulsive, and less inclined to adhere to morally guided behavior.

THE IMMORAL SELF

To appreciate how the diminished self falls prey to immoral behavior, we need only consider our own bad little habits, those things we would rather do less frequently or to a lesser extent. A few of mine include eating a pint of frozen yogurt all at once, procrastination of healthy activities such as exercise, and, more seriously, too often becoming distracted while my wife is talking. For many people, such a list might include drinking three beers instead of one, watching TV shows in which they have no genuine interest, spending too much money shopping, or hurting the feelings of loved ones. The crucial question becomes: *When are we more likely to succumb to these habits, when we feel powerful and good about ourselves, or when racked with guilt, shame, anxiety, or anger?*

The relentless assault on cognitive processes, including moral judgment, has always been the problem of guilt-based, shame-enforced morality, especially in a population, like attachment abusers, suffering from a diminished sense of self with low self-esteem. (Kegan, 1982, even suggests that poor moral development may result in these and other narcissistic or impaired-self symptoms.) The diminished self can do little to control impulses or make sound moral judgments, and, therefore, functions unreliably as a moral agent. At best, self-eroding shame leads to fearful compliance and secretiveness, not to the development of compassion (Gilbert, 1989, 1992, 1994).

Shame and compassion are incompatible. The former

locks us in a state of self-obsession in which other people are merely sources of affect, whereas the latter requires taking the perspectives of others. In most cases of attachment abuse, the problem is not the force of the abusive impulse but the break down of the normal safeguard against abuse: compassion. We discovered this clinically in a dramatic way by treating several groups of child sexual abusers. It became clear in their detailed descriptions of their subjective experience that the shame of sexual arousal stimulated by attraction to a child encapsulates the abuser in a narcissistic shell. Thus insulated from accurate processing of social cues and unmediated by prosocial inhibitions, the temporarily empowering sexual impulse grows stronger (as a means of pain-relief and self-enhancement); whereas internal controls, under the assault of shame, weaken, permitting objectification of the victim as nothing more than a source of affect. We taught these clients to apply *HEALS* (the emotional regulation technique based on self-compassion—see next chapter) to the shame of arousal. ("Having sexual feelings doesn't mean I'm a bad person.") Immediately, the shame abated, breaking the narcissistic shell and allowing the abuser to take the perspective of the potential victim. Now he could see that sexual behavior with a child would ruin the attachment relationship and do serious harm to the child. Pain-relieving compassion was stimulated, simultaneously *reducing sexual arousal.*

Researchers are beginning to appreciate the link between the shame-diminished self and abuse, with the implication that shaming methods of treatment are more likely to increase rage and narcissistic styles than reduce them (Gilbert, 1992, 1994; Lansky, 1987; Lewis, 1971, 1976, 1989; Retzinger, 1991; Scheff, 1989, 1990; Tangney, 1991, 1992). Indeed, high levels of shame and related anxiety and anger are likely to yield recidivism of undesired behavior (Litman, Eiser, Rawson, & Oppenheim, 1979; Marlatt & Gordon, 1985; Neidigh et al., 1988; Neidigh & Tomiko, 1991; Potter-Efron & Potter-Efron, 1991). There is growing awareness that the surge of violence and tendency toward narcissistic behaviors widely noted in contemporary society involves, as

Gilbert (1994) puts it, the trivialization of prosocial motivations such as compassion and forgiveness (Levenson, 1992; Smail, 1987). Ours is a shaming culture (Broucek, 1991; Nathanson, 1992). We may well find that this is the cause, rather than the result, of the much discussed culture of violence.

THE MORAL SELF

Eisenburg and Mussen (1989), in reviewing research on the promotion of prosocial behavior in children, developed a list of important contributing factors that include: personal competency and general well-being, reinforcement of prosocial behavior by role models, experiencing benefits of prosocial behavior, and having opportunities to practice prosocial conflict resolution. These are necessary components of any treatment to bring about the powerful sense of self that makes moral agency possible. The powerful self enjoys self-enhancement through the act of declining the second beer or the bowl of frozen yogurt. Parents with powerful selves respond to disrespectful children with compassionate instruction rather than angry counter-attack; they empower a spouse or child or elder parent (instead of engaging in power struggles) and thereby achieve a degree of internal power far greater than that available in imposing one's will on a loved one. *The incarnation of moral agency lies in the fortified sense of self provided by compassion for self and loved ones.*

THE REWARDS OF SELF-COMPASSION

- emotional regulation
- defense from emotional abuse
- self-esteem
- personal dignity
- compassion for loved ones
- social-relatedness

Self-compassion provides regulation of internal experience and serves as an incompatible response to antisocial behavior. It dissipates the narcissistic shell that encapsulates us within our own emotional experience and blinds us to the feelings of others. It protects us from emotional abuse at the hands of others by preventing internalization of abuse; any abusive behavior by others is seen as a reflection of *their* internal state and not as an indictment of the self. The enhanced degree of self-regulation provided by self-compassion increases self-esteem and well-being, affording a greater sense of genuine personal dignity, predicated on respect for the personal dignity of others. It allows the self-enhancing experience of shame-free compassion for others, enriching attachment relationships in particular and social relatedness in general. Self-compassion builds personal boundaries through personal definition and differentiation. Emerging from within, these self-developed boundaries cannot function as barriers to intimacy, care-giving, nurturance, and other prosocial behavior, inasmuch as the experience of self-compassion entails acceptance of these as basic human needs, the fulfillment of which the self is capable and worthy.

SELF-COMPASSION AND MORAL DEVELOPMENT

Edward Gondolf (1987) was among the first authors to apply developmental theory to attachment abusers, using Kohlberg's (1981) model of moral development to describe violent spouse abusers. Kohlberg's theory outlines a sequence of stages, through which individuals move toward higher moral development, albeit greatly influenced by environmental contingencies. Extending Piaget's (1932/1965) theory of moral reasoning as a subclass of cognitive development, Kohlberg postulated six stages of moral reasoning, divided into three levels of development. In level 1, the preconventional, children justify actions as right or wrong on the basis of whether they lead to pleasurable or punitive consequences. In stage 2 they develop awareness of differing moral points of view. However, these are tempered by the concrete belief that everyone acts to ensure his/her own physical comfort. Level II introduces conventional awareness, with a new regard of conformity to social rules as the basis for morality. But now rules are upheld for their own sake, rather than for the consequences of breaking them. Stage 3 is known as the "good boy/good girl" orientation. Here the individual wants to maintain attachment affection by projecting the presumed persona of a good kid; morality is a means of securing affection. In stage 4, the individual transcends the dyadic or attachment boundaries and generalizes the importance of social order and justice. Here rules must be obeyed and authority deferred to, regardless of the circumstances or the individuals involved. Level III is the arena of postconventional or principled reasoning. Here individuals move beyond unquestioning acceptance of the moral principles of their culture and make an effort to define morality in terms of abstract principles and values that are valid in all situations in all societies. Stage 6 is the universal ethical principle orientation. Here ethical principles are comprehensive, rational, and universally applicable. Individuals make ethical decisions by simultaneously considering the perspectives of all parties in a moral dilemma and choosing which role they could endorse were they in the dilemma.

Gondolf's adaptation of Kohlberg's six stages creates descriptions familiar to most clinicians who deal with attachment abusers of any kind. He divides developmental stages into two levels: denial and behavioral change. The first includes defiance and self-justification of abuse, in which moral reasoning is narcissistic and in which continued abuse is virtually assured. The second level, behavioral change, begins with stage 3, in which the abuser realizes that he has victimized himself along with his attachment figures. Abuse is likely to continue in this stage, as narcissistic entitlement persists. In the relationship-building stage, the abuser's growing awareness of his own feelings enables him to recognize the feelings of others. This new level of empathy awakens still further feelings in the self through emotional reciprocity. However, relapse remains a high risk, unless the abuser develops regulatory skills for the higher and broader emotional expression he now experiences. Stage 5 is described as a community-service stage, in which the abuser becomes interested in the internal value of his compassion for others. In stage 6, the abuser begins to adopt broad ethical principles with regard to human dignity and a just society.

One obvious problem with developmental stages of moral reasoning is that they do not preclude recidivism of immoral behavior. The numbers of attachment abusers capable of sophisticated moral reasoning attest to this. Every clinician who has worked with abusers knows that a great many are committed to community service and high social principles. Many are well-meaning and, in general, moral persons whose ethical failings have come from the failure of self-compassion, which inevitably blunts their compassion for specific others (namely victims) even while maintaining commendable compassion for humanity-at-large. Virtually every court-ordered group for violent child and spouse abusers I have led has had an ordained minister mandated into treatment. I have also led groups of highly sophisticated Catholic priests who have sexually abused children. It was not the level of moral reasoning that distinguished these abusers from non-abusers but the shame-diminished self that, in effect, made the perpetrators feel *unworthy* of the internal rewards of moral behavior and which numbed them to the vulnerabilities of their victims. It may be that the clergy specifically, and persons whose moral reasoning can be described by Kohlberg's advanced stages in general, are susceptible to moral failings whenever a diminished sense of self confuses the virtue of humility with the symptom of low self-esteem. The loathed self, it seems, finds ways to do loathsome things. In any case, movement from one stage to another in the Kohlberg/Gondolf model depends on two factors: the ability of abusers to regulate internal experience and protect the self from perceived emotional attacks from others, through heavy doses of self-compassion, that in turn enable them to feel compassion for others. In the Compassion Workshop, morality functions as a therapeutic device (a pathway to self-esteem) to enhance personal well-being.

TEACHING COMPASSIONATE MORALITY TO SEVERE ABUSERS

We know from research that a significant number of severely violent abusers, those presumably in stage 1 of Gondolf's adaptation, are generally assaultive. The ranks of attachment abusers include narcissistic and antisocial personality disorders, and a special subclass that Jacobson (1993) calls "vagal reactors," who seem to function physiologically at their best when they are most cruel. These are men who achieve their deepest concentration when paying back the world for its many transgressions. What chance do clinicians, in private practice or in structured groups, have of teaching these persons compassionate morality?

The answer returns us to the heart of the relationship between shame, anger, and morality. It has been argued here and elsewhere (Gilbert, 1994; Levenson, 1992; Smail, 1987) that the trivialization of prosocial emotions, such as compassion and forgiveness, contributes to the development of sociopathy. It would seem then that the enhancement of prosocial emotions can help build an internal sense of self sufficiently solid to serve as the basis on which to construct moral agency (Gilbert, 1994; Miedzian, 1992; Miller & Eisenberg, 1988) and replace the transitory self-righteousness that, at least momentarily, justifies violence in the mind of the abuser (Katz, 1988). Such transformation is possible so long as the treatment emphasizes the development of self-compassion as a mechanism of self-regulation and self-enhancement. Acquisition of these learnable skills affords the most difficult of abusers, often for the first time in their lives, the experience of internal power independent of transitory feelings states. It exposes them to the possibility of interpersonal empowerment with a far greater sense of personal power than destructiveness can offer them.

Of course, genuine power must be distinguished in the minds of clients from destructiveness. The illusory feeling of power experienced while thinking or acting destructively comes from a temporary feelings state serving to fill-in gaping holes in the self. As the feelings state wanes, the inflated sense of self greatly diminishes. Abusers must learn that a stable sense of internal power rises only from self-compassion and compassion for others. The 8-minute dramatic video, *Compassion*, models this point by dramatizing an altercation in which a man is about to beat his wife. He uses *H*EALS to apply self-compassion and compassion for his spouse. Client-viewers have no doubt of when he is more powerful.

But even with zealous effort, it has been our experience in the Compassion Workshop that, with many of the severe abusers described above (about 15%–25% of the total), the best we can hope for is that they come to use the techniques they learn in treatment to mimic compassion, or even to use the techniques as yet another tactic, albeit a nonviolent one, in controlling family members. However short of ideal expectations these options seem, they are better for victims and child witnesses, as well as abusers, than violence and intimidation. Many persons in this subpopulation need more systematic self-building treatment than the Compassion Workshop can provide, such as that described in *The Powerful Self* (Stosny, 1994). But a treatment emphasizing self-compassion at least has a shot at changing severe abusers. Human beings never voluntarily relinquish external power unless they feel internally powerful. Nor do they become consistently moral unless they transcend the pseudomoral justification they construct in acts of revenge, retaliation, and punishment. Therein lies the challenge and the duty in treatment of attachment abusers.

CHAPTER SUMMARY

Ethical treatment of attachment abusers is informed by a theory of moral agency. Moral behavior can have external motivations, in the form of rewards and sanctions in the environment, or internal motivations of positive (compassion) or negative (guilt, shame, abandonment anxiety) valence. A person with a powerful sense of self is far more able to behave morally and is far less susceptible to impulsiveness and abuse of self or others; moral agency and prosocial behavior seem a function of a powerful sense of self fortified by self-compassion. The experience of self-compassion provides self-regulation and serves as an incompatible response to antisocial and immoral behavior. Thus therapeutic enhancement of compassion for self makes it possible to move with relative rapidity through what has been described as the higher stages of moral development. In the Compassion Workshop, the subject of morality, presented as a vital component of self-esteem, serves as a therapeutic mechanism to enhance personal well-being.

Part II

Treating Attachment Abuse

7 The Compassion Workshop, Module One: Healing

The Compassion Workshop consists of structured treatment modules for all forms of attachment abuse at any level along the continuum of abuse (Figure I.3, p. vi). The treatment seeks to provide remedial self-building that creates internally motivated moral and prosocial behavior. In each of its treatment modules, compassion serves as an incompatible response to negative affect in general and to anger, aggression, and abuse in particular. Compassion also serves as an interpersonal enhancement of the attachment bond. In treating attachment abusers, clinicians must not forget that emotional arousal numbs the pain that stimulates it. In asking clients to give up pain relievers, while providing them with no other, we differ little from primitive dentists gouging at exposed nerves without anesthetic. Fortunately, the salient attachment emotion serves as a viable anesthetic, as well as a balm of healing.

COMPASSION AS PSYCHIATRIC NOVOCAINE

The use of compassion as dissipator of anger and aggression has empirical support in the work of Baron (1976, 1979, 1983, 1984). Baron has shown that provoked subjects become less hostile toward their tormentors after a pleasant experience, even if the pleasant experience is irrelevant to the provocative one. In other words, "feeling better" dissipates the anger-arousal response that leads to aggression and violence. The apposite behavioral technique is *incompatible response strategy*, based on a well-established principle of behavior: Human beings are incapable of engaging in two incompatible responses at once (e.g., Baron, 1984; Wolpe, 1958). Inducing reactions incompatible with anger-aggression, such as compassion or empathy, dissipates anger and aggression (Baron, 1984; Miller & Eisenberg, 1988; Whiteman, Fanshel, & Grundy, 1987). The more empathy or compassion we feel, the less anger we feel. Furthermore, the experience of compassion and prosocial behavior can be learned and has been demonstrated to be trainable (Eisenburg & Mussen, 1989; MacDonald, 1988). The importance of training abusers in compassion and prosocial behavior looms as utterly crucial. Gilbert (1994) suggests that the problem of violence is less a matter of too much of something (e.g., anger, aggression, exertion of power and control, negative attitudes toward women and children) than of too little of something, namely, compassion, moral judgment, and relationship skills (Miedzian, 1992). In the Compassion Workshop, clients learn the skill to stimulate the incompatible response of compassion for the purpose of dissipating anger or anxiety arousal before it leads to aggression. The treatment not only helps clients develop the skill of identifying and labeling the feelings that trigger anger arousal, it trains them to convert the trigger feelings to the more pleasant experience of compassion for themselves and for the prospective victims of their abuse.

COMPASSION AND SELF-CONSTRUCTIONS

By virtue of its cognitive component (understanding the deeper experience of another), compassion serves as a tool for changing the negative self-constructions that give rise to abuse. This function of compassion works in two ways. First, it changes the way feedback from attachment figures is perceived, through a deeper understanding of attachment figures. In other words, attachment figures are seen as more than confirmation of, or contradiction to, distorted self-constructions. The second way that compassion alters self-constructions is more profound. With deeper understanding of the self, distorted self-constructions give way to reality.

ATTITUDES BASED ON IGNORANCE VERSUS ATTITUDES BASED ON SELF-CONSTRUCTIONS

The Compassion Workshop virtually ignores obvious social attitudes while seeking to change deeper meaning structures. Research indicates that merely changing situational behavior runs the risk of increasing physical abuse, at least in certain types of abusers (Gondolf, 1988; Hamberger & Hastings, 1988a) or increasing psychological abuse even as physical abuse wanes (Hamberger & Hastings, 1988b; Saunders & Azar, 1989). From a treatment standpoint, social attitudes are the most superficial facet of an individual's belief system. They reflect self-constructions while having no causal effect on them. As such they serve merely as excuses and rationalizations for certain behaviors. For instance, it may seem to an abuser that he slaps his wife for failing to have his dinner ready when he wants it. This impression comes from the false meaning he assigns to the behavior of his spouse as a result of his own self-constructions. He has constructed an attachment landscape, in which data supporting his deep belief that he is unlovable receive priority processing to the point of reality distortion. Accordingly, his wife's behavior *means* to him that he is unlovable, and he punishes her for reminding him of the painful burden he holds deep within himself. His attitudes about male privilege or the duties of a wife, however repulsive, do not cause the abuse. Confronting the social attitude without changing the self-construction from which it is derived and of which it is a superficial reflection will never succeed in stopping abuse, albeit, in conjunction with legal sanctions for violence, it sometimes changes the form and nature of abuse. In contrast, altering self-constructions to provide a sense of internal power (making the exertion of external power unnecessary) will change social attitudes without directly assaulting the least strategically important but most well-defended outpost of the meaning-system.[1]

There may be one area of attitude alteration that can produce positive behavioral change in attachment relationships. Attitudes based on ignorance, such as construing a 2-year-old's contrariness as a personal affront, rather than the result of a natural and healthy developmental phase, might be dispelled by pertinent information on child development. But even here, the self-constructions that underlie adult feelings of rejection or devaluation, in response to the behavior of a young child, remains a stagnant pool from which the miasma of abuse can scarcely fail to emanate.

CONJOINT TREATMENT OF ABUSERS AND VICTIMS

The fundamental purpose of the Compassion Workshop—to ameliorate the disordered self-building function of attachment relationships—affords the flexibility to work for both abusers and victims, either separately or in conjoint sessions. Both victims and abusers need help in the area of toxic blame. The abuser blames his internal states on the victim, rendering himself powerless over his own internal experience, whereas the victim internalizes blame for the internal state of the abuser, rendering herself powerless to heal the wounded self. Treating attachment figures conjointly has the advantage of helping individuals internalize responsibility for their own experience and for no one else's. The therapist actively helps set boundaries of self-responsibility by pointing out the power that responsibility gives each individual, whereas blame creates nothing but a sense of powerlessness.

---

[1]Unfortunately, most existent treatments for abusers reinforce their self-constructions of unlovability, thereby inflaming the cause of abuse.

SELECTING, PROCESSING, AND PACING THE HANDOUTS

The Compassion Workshop offers a generic treatment for deficits that impair affect-regulation and viable negotiation of attachment relationships. The fundamental properties of the Workshop make possible a wide application to fit the range of attachment abusers and their victims, which contains great variation. Some will need little or no preparation to get right to the skill-building aspects of the treatment, whereas others will need to be seduced into the self-enhancement value of the Workshop handouts. It certainly is not expected that every client will need every handout that follows nor that every handout is appropriate for every client. One enormous advantage of treating attachment abuse by individual cases, as opposed to structured groups for primary, secondary, or tertiary prevention, is that individual therapists are able to make more accurate assessments and treatment planning.

The primary guides for selecting handouts to process for given clients should be score on the Conflict Tactics Scale (CTS, Straus, 1979) (above the norm for verbal aggression and *any* incidence of physical aggression), elevated anger, hostility and/or anxiety scores on a symptom questionnaire, a lower than normal score on the Attachment Compassion Scale, and any deficits in perspective-taking, sympathy for self and loved ones, validation of the emotional experience of self and loved ones, or emotional vocabulary.

Obviously, clinicians are most qualified to know which handouts to select for which clients, which to process in therapy sessions or to be given for reading at home, and how to pace the introduction of handouts. Sometimes processing will be accomplished optimally by reading through the handout aloud as clients read along. Sometimes a didactic presentation hitting the main points of handouts and asking socratic questions about them will work best. And sometimes asking clients to question whether the main points of the handouts illuminate some aspect of their experience will produce the best results. Of course, the personality and personal style of individual therapists will do much to determine how handouts are processed. As long as the focus remains on the self-building aspect of treatment, therapists can scarcely go wrong in the way they choose to process any given handout.

Note: The sample handouts that follow are assembled for those clients who either don't know they're in abusive relationships or who don't believe that the abuse is their most important problem. Specialized workbooks for court-ordered spouse, child, and elder abusers as well as Prevention Manuals, are available from Intermedia, 1-800-553-8336. The manuals are client-ready, with illustrations.

MODULE ONE: HEALING

If a client is suspected of attachment abuse, a safety contract, such as that depicted in Worksheet 7.1, should be executed at the beginning of treatment. In exchange for a promise of prosocial behavior, the safety contract assures the personal rewards of internal power, well-being, and pride. This sets the morality-as-self-building tone of the Compassion Workshop.

Once the safety contract is signed (or deemed unnecessary), clients are given a copy of the Bill of Rights and Peace Agreement (Worksheet 7.2). Of course, some clients will question the rationale for the admonishment not to discuss hot issues, which are the very things that brought them to treatment in the first place. Explain, compassionately, that hurtful issues inevitably surface in therapy and that a great many people go home and have terrible fights about the content of the sessions. For the well-being of everyone involved, it's important to learn emotional regulation techniques before discussing painful topics. This will facilitate the gains of therapy without risk of harm. Worksheet 7.3 offers clients a diagrammatic rationale for this important safety issue.

If severe emotional abuse or violence is admitted, temporary emergency tactics, such as those in Worksheet 7.4, should be put into operation until the ***HEALS*** technique is learned. However, clinicians should take care to stress the temporary nature of item #6. Time-outs resolve and heal nothing, and are, in that sense, antithetical to the Compassion Workshop.

Don't worry about giving out your home phone number as an emergency number. I have found that attachment abusers and victims, most of whom suffer external locus of control, need to know that they have a resource outside themselves to set parameters on their behavior, even though they *seldom* use it. I get no more than three or four late-night calls per year from the nearly 200 clients who go through the Compassion Workshop.

HOMEWORK ASSIGNMENTS

The Compassion Workshop makes abundant use of homework assignments. Collectively these develop an additional dimension of treatment in the form of written dialogue between therapist and client. This continually emergent dimension helps clients to feel like participants in the treatment even outside the sessions. When going over the homework (Worksheets 7.5 and 7.6) be sure that clients have given sufficient thought to the phenomenological details of their experience of anger. They should think in terms of specific sensations and arousal, to set the stage for the vital labelling process that serves as the foundation of their developing regulatory skills. Illiterate clients should be helped verbally to compile and discuss their individual lists.

Make certain that clients are behavior-specific in listing what they need to do to accomplish their goals. Superficial responses like, "Be different," or, "Sit through the sessions," or, "Allow my spouse (or children) to change," are obviously unacceptable. Adequate thought to whatever changes in themselves their goals demand should be clearly in evidence in the responses. If this is not the case, rigorous processing within the session is necessary.

GOALS

In cases involving attachment abuse, goal-setting in treatment takes on special significance. Both abusers and victims tend to be reactive rather than proactive and external in locus of control rather than internal. Goal-setting helps to reverse both tendencies. All goals should be viable, that is, achievable with some challenge but not superior effort. When going over Worksheet 7.7, emphasize that long-term, intermediate, and short-term goals work together for maximal efficiency, fitting into a larger context of primary, over-riding goals. In keeping with the philosophy of the Compassion Workshop, the primary, overriding goals are the first legs of the continuum of abuse (Figure I.3, p. vi). To reinforce client commitment to the primary, overriding goal, the therapist should ask all clients to state their goals *aloud.* I always make light of the manipulative quality of this: "We know from research that people make greater commitment to a goal if they state it aloud in public. This goal is so important to your well-being that I don't mind being manipulative about it."

POWER

The notion of power as a feeling *within,* rather than something to be sought from others or imposed on others, must be established early in treatment. The first step of gaining internal power comes from awareness of internal experience, as described in Worksheet 7.8.

Worksheet 7.9 advances the conception of anger as a transitory and false power, lasting only so long as arousal lasts. It also pictures the family of feelings included under the umbrella of anger, differentiated, one from the other, by the degree of arousal each commands. This helps clients accurately assess how much arousal they associate with each feeling, a vital asset in the development of regulatory skills. The handout reinforces the importance of self-awareness as the key to genuine power.

The special place occupied by resentment in Worksheet 7.9 will be discussed later in the treatment. For now clients need to know that resentment creates a plateau of anger arousal, keeping the cycle going for long periods of time. In other words, the presence of resentment keeps us partially aroused much of the time, so that the occurrence of anger-trigger events have little room for increased arousal before reaching dangerous high points; the persistence of resentment has the effect of shortening the fuse of anger.

THE ANGER–AROUSAL CYCLE

Clients are now prepared for the series of handouts on the effects of anger arousal. Combined in Worksheet 7.10, these cover the damage that frequent anger arousal does to the body, mind, and spirit. Anger arousal distorts the true self and eventually exacerbates the painful feelings of powerlessness that stimulated the arousal in the first place. Thus anger is self-perpetuating.

THE LINK BETWEEN HURT AND COMPASSION

Unlike the association of hurt with anger, which causes greater damage to self and loved ones, the connection between hurt and compassion heals. (See Worksheet 7.11.) Where anger is a cry of powerlessness, compassion provides a feeling of genuine power.

Worksheet 7.12 describes compassion as a triadic experience, with cognitive, affective, and behavioral components. This handout should deepen client conception of compassion as a healing agent with inherent self-reward.

STIMULATING THE EXPERIENCE OF COMPASSION

Many clients need exposure to the healing power of compassion early in treatment. The video, *Shadows of the Heart,* was made for this purpose. The video presentation sets a vital tone for the treatment, by organizing the diffuse sense of self of abusers and victims around the feelings of pride and self-esteem they gain through the experience of compassion. The video depicts spouse abuse through the eyes of a child who feels responsible for his mother's pain. Clients are instructed to focus on the child and to think of how they can protect him. This invokes a form of compassion that has survival-based importance to the species: rescuing children from imminent peril. Worksheet 7.13 sets up the video.

In setting up the video, be sure to focus attention on the child, to assure a compassionate response. Our experience in developing the video was that focusing attention on the parents produced a strong reaction of anger. If attention is centered on the child, however, the compassionate response is generalized to include the parents. Though it is only speculation, it seemed to us that having compassion for the child allowed clients to understand that the hurt causing abusive behavior can be ameliorated (Stosny, 1994). This knowledge renders anger arousal unnecessary.

Made with professional actors, *Shadows of the Heart* depicts an abuser, who, as is typical of abusers, feels coerced into treatment. Humiliated and overtly angry, he presents the therapist and a peer-counselor with formidable resistance. The character's anger and humiliation validates the feelings of many client viewers, while dramatizing what anger-motivated behavior looks like. (To acquire the video, call Intermedia, 1-800-533-8336.)

Worksheet 7.14 contains postprocessing notes for the video. These should be done as a homework assignment. (If the video is shown as part of the treatment session, questions 1–3 should be discussed immediately after viewing the video.) The therapist should direct attention to how much better the experience of compassion feels, compared to anger. It is a good idea to make this a somatic comparison as well as a psychological one. Ask clients to consider the difference in their eyes, jaws, neck, shoulders, chest, and stomach. The purpose of this segment of treatment is to implant the notion that clients can choose the rewards of a compassionate response over the pain of reactive anger.

Worksheet 7.15 introduces the notion that compassion is synonymous with assertiveness, due to its compelling behavioral component to change false meaning about the self and to give support to loved ones to change false meanings about themselves. The handout shows the difference between arousal of compassion and anger. The former does not suffer the precipitous decline into guilt, shame, and depression of the latter. Instead, compassion creates well-being and boosts self-esteem, keeping spirits elevated for extended periods of time.

The Golden Rule of Internal Power (Worksheet 7.16) cautions clients against taking vulnerable feelings to loved ones for regulation. An important precursor to abusive behavior, external regulation of affect is framed as antithetical to genuine power.

PREPARING CLIENTS FOR *H*EALS

Worksheet 7.17 depicts the interaction of effort and reward in learning *H*EALS. *H*EALS is an acronym for the word, "Healing" visualized in flashing letters; "Explain to yourself" the deepest of the core hurts; "Apply Self-Compassion" by changing the meaning of the core hurts; "Love yourself," and "Solve the problem." It is important to emphasize that the deliberate, sometimes arduous, effort in learning the skill to do *H*EALS is only temporary, lasting about 2 or 3 weeks, before it becomes easy and second nature. From the first successful try, a deeper feeling of self-control increases well-being. Soon the resulting freedom from emotional reactivity creates interpersonal consequences as clients learn to de-escalate negative emotional exchanges. Within 3 weeks of practicing *H*EALS, the vast majority of clients feel much better than at the beginning of treatment.

Worksheet 7.18 introduces *H*EALS with important information about the varying amounts of effort individuals need to exert in developing the skill. In one of the early groups of the Compassion Workshop, a former professional basketball player likened *H*EALS to learning a new way of shooting foul shots. "You have to hold your hands all funny," he said. "But once you learn it, you hit a lot more foul shots." Looking within the self to regulate internal experience is the equivalent, in the eyes of many attachment abusers, of "holding your hands all funny." A basketball player has to practice shooting foul shots over and over again, to maintain the "right feeling" in his hands. Only then can he consistently make foul shots without thinking about each step of the shooting process. This is how the skill of emotional regulation works, once *H*EALS is practiced until it "just *feels* right."

Working like a vaccination, *H*EALS raises tolerance of, and sensitivity to, core vulnerable hurts. When we're vaccinated against a disease, a very small dose of the disease is injected into the blood stream to stimulate the immune system to create disease-preventing antibodies. *H*EALS exposes clients to very small doses of the core vulnerable feelings that cause powerful negative experience. The technique stimulates the central nervous system to build a regulatory function that eases the pain of negative experience. Tolerance of the core feelings increases, whereas sensitivity to them diminishes. As a consequence, clients are less easily hurt, insulted, and provoked. With internalized regulation, they are less apt to blame their feelings on attachment figures. Most important, they learn to convert negative emotion into self-building experience.

HEALS

*H*EALS (Worksheet 7.19), the core of a technology of self-building, is a technique of self-regulation, that is, alteration of meaning dominated by negative affect, such as anger, anxiety, shame, and guilt, to adjust the degree, intensity, and valence of emotional experience. The means of self-regulation specific to *H*EALS is the habitually manipulated experience of compassion for self and loved ones.

*H*EALS begins when the client imagines the brightly colored letters, "HEALING," flashing three or four times. This step of *H*EALS represents more than mere thought-stopping, itself a proven technique in reduction of emotional arousal (e.g., Williams & Williams, 1993). The flashing letters also serve as the sort of mental imagery that has been shown to stimulate the body's natural healing mechanisms (Levine, Gordon, & Fields, 1978; McMahon & Sheikh, 1984; Meichenbaum, 1977; Rider, 1985; Sheikh & Jordan, 1983). More important, the technique constitutes an incompatible response to anger, hostility, and aggression. The organism cannot think, "heal," and, at the same time, feel hostility or behave aggressively.

The "explain to yourself" step of *H*EALS involves self-validation of anger-trigger feelings. "Self-validation" means acknowledgment of the construction of meaning as part of one's internal reality at that moment. Once experienced, for just a few seconds, the construction can be changed more easily (Daldrup, Beutler, Engle, & Greenburg, 1988). When clients express anger-trigger feelings orally and in writing, dominant processing transfers from mid-brain–limbic (emotional) to front-brain–cerebral cortex (cognitive), which is an efficient, if not the most natural, way for the developing brain to regulate affective experience (Berkowitz, 1990; Dodge, 1991; Dunn & Brown, 1991).

The "apply self-compassion" step of *H*EALS enables clients to change the negative meaning about the self to which their defenses and symptoms are in reaction. Incompatible response strategy is invoked once again in the "love yourself" step of *H*EALS. No one can feel unlovable, powerless over internal experience, unacceptable, worthless, untrustworthy, or unimportant, while experiencing genuine compassion. Clients will initially draw a blank on this, however, for no one really knows *how* to feel lovable. It helps to ask them to consider which qualities come to mind when they think of a lovable person. If they continue to draw a blank, ask if a lovable person is someone who is totally involved in his or her own interests and concerns without caring about anyone else. Eventually they'll volunteer that the qualities of a lovable person are various forms of compassion. When we feel compassion, we feel worthy of love.

Worksheet 7.20 describes further how *H*EALS functions like a vaccination. It gives detailed instructions for step two of *H*EALS, experiencing the core feeling that causes the target symptom. It also suggests how and where to practice the technique.

An entire treatment session should be spent practicing *H*EALS. Get clients to recall a recent event that angered or upset them. They will need to be walked through each step of *H*EALS as often as necessary to experience emotional relief. For most people this will take two or three tries, with exceptions noted below.

PROBLEMS WITH *H*EALS

When *H*EALS doesn't work for clients, it is almost always because they did not go low enough on the list of core hurts. *H*EALS works if a client goes too low, for instance, saying, "I feel unlovable," when the core hurt is merely a sense of unimportance. But it will *not* work if the client, for example, says, "I feel devalued," when he/she is actually feeling unlovable. So the general rule is: Go lower than the client believes his hurt to be, with the following exception. Some clients have trouble experiencing even a few seconds of the core hurts, particularly if depression or psychic pain is too great. Such clients need gentle support and additional help to realize that they will not only survive the momentary experience of these feelings, but that their brief experience in the context of therapy will heal them.

Alexithymic clients may need to somatize the core hurts, in something like, "I feel tight in the shoulders, a pit in the stomach, an empty feeling." The healing process occurs when the core hurts are converted into thought and language, where they are subject to higher-level cognitive processing. Ultimately, it matters not to the process *which* word-forms the core hurts take, so long as they are made linguistic.

Many clients will invent their own words for the core hurts, such as "I feel disrespected," or "I feel like shit." Of course this is okay and should be encouraged, especially when cultural differences are indicated.

Many clients, usually anger-junkies, don't want to give up the temporary power of anger arousal. Therapists should perceive this as a fervent cry of powerlessness that will be relieved only with validation of the client's deeper experience that causes the anger-arousal. The strategy is not to inflame or refortify defensive anger, but to make it unnecessary through provision of more viable defenses, such as those inherent in the experience of compassion. Admittedly, the process will be longer with clients heavily invested in their anger. But these are the very clients whose need for compassionate treatment is most acute.

Worksheet 7.21 shows the weekly log for practice of *H*EALS. This sort of self monitoring is necessary to inspire adequate practice repetitions of the technique. Only if practiced repeatedly, can *H*EALS help restore the self-building function of attachment relationships.

Even if physical abuse is not considered a threat, the category should remain on the log, if only to spur more candid response to the hurt-feelings category.

Worksheet 7.22 shows the weekly Scale of Internal Power. This is yet another self-monitoring technique to give clients a concrete measure of how well they are doing. In my experience, virtually every client shows sharply declining values for numbers 1–8 and increasing ones for item 9.

Worksheet 7.1

The Compassion Workshop Building Genuine Pride

GOALS: POWER WITHIN

Over the next few weeks, you will learn positive and pleasant ways to regulate feelings, beliefs, and behavior. Learning and practicing these new skills will enhance your sense of self. Your self-esteem will grow through the experience of genuine pride and compassion.

Agreement to be Compassionate

Your signature on this agreement obligates you to make a supreme effort to be compassionate with family members and significant others. This includes refraining from criticism of personalities, attacking self-esteem, insulting or name-calling, controlling or manipulating, coercing, threatening or intimidating, destroying property, hitting, or any unwanted touching. As you learn new emotional regulation skills, it will become increasingly easy, and pleasurable to refrain from these behaviors.

Signature:

(Give this document to your therapist.)

Therapist:

Worksheet 7.2

Bill of Rights and Peace Agreement

No one, under any circumstances, deserves to be disregarded, insulted, controlled, intimidated, hurt, hit, pushed, grabbed, or touched in *any* undesired way.

Nothing that anyone in a family says or does justifies abuse. *One act of abuse never justifies another.*

Abuse of loved ones becomes something we're scarcely aware of, like a bad habit. Once established, bad habits are hard to unlearn.

Until new, healthier habits are learned, a *temporary* non-discussion agreement is necessary.

1. Don't talk about hot issues.

    a. Don't ignore them either. Make a list of them as they occur, and save them until you've learned new skills to discuss them without the danger of abuse.
    b. If you feel you absolutely must discuss hot issues in the relationship, agree on one half hour per day and no more than that.

2. Discuss with one another what you learn in treatment. But limit your discussion to techniques and process—*how* you communicate, not *what* you communicate. There will be plenty of time to talk about issues once you really know how to do it.
3. Recognize that some confusion and anxiety are normal in the recovery process. They are temporary conditions that will pass as you learn more and develop greater skill.

Worksheet 7.3

The Path to Problem Resolution

Or Why We Can't Deal with Hot Issues Yet

FAMILY PROBLEM

money
inconvenience
disappointment

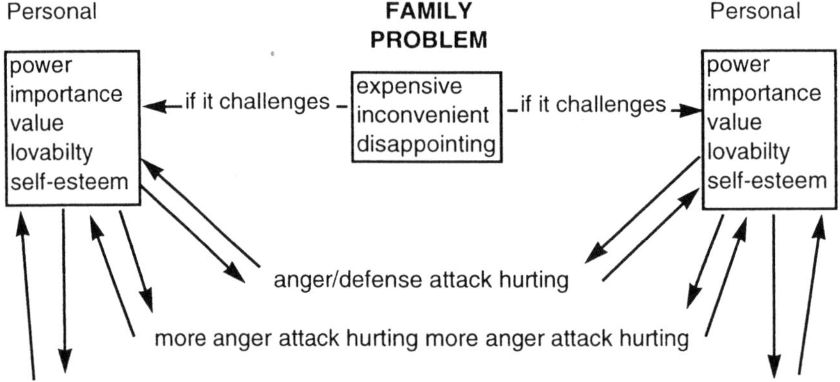

Once the problem is seen as an attack on the self, hurt is experienced, which causes anger, which leads to an attack on the attachment figure, who, hurt and angry, counter-attacks. Now the dispute is no longer about the problem that started it. Now the fight is over the injuries done to the self. It will be impossible to solve the problem because no solution to the problem will resolve the injuries to self and to loved ones, which, after the fight, may be expressed as resentment, hidden hostility, and anger at trivial things.

A person's sense of self is *never* realistically at stake in problems of expense, inconvenience, and disappointment.

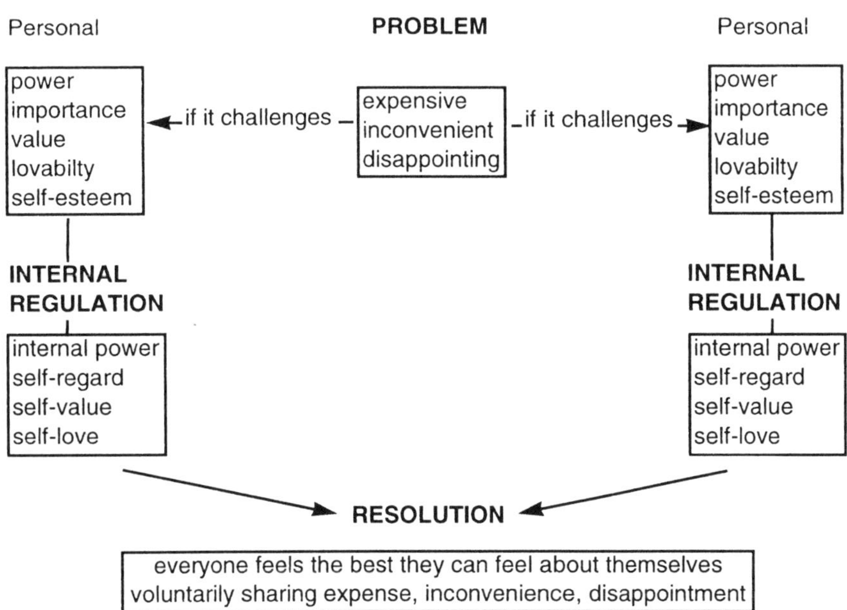

Once hurt and anger enter into it, the path to resolution *must* pass through Internal Regulation. No problem and no behavior of another person can possibly diminish your internal power, your importance, value, lovabilty, and self-esteem, unless you allow it to do so by giving it a *false meaning.*

The Internal Regulation process eliminates false meanings and converts hurtful, negative experience into positive, growth-oriented experience, making the next step, problem *resolution*, not only possible, but, most of the time, easy.

Worksheet 7.4

Emergency Tactics

No matter what the circumstances, people always feel bad after they've hurt someone they care about. To avoid that bad feeling, to avoid hurting yourself and those you love, use the following emergency tactics.

EMERGENCY TACTICS

1. Know your early anger-danger signs (what anger feels like in your head, your eyes, your mouth, neck, shoulders, chest, back, and hands).
2. Anger is caused by hurt. Know that when you and your loved ones are angry, you're really hurt. Focus on the hurt, not the anger. Why are you hurt? Why is he or she hurt? *How can you make it better?*
3. Try to communicate about the hurt, not about the anger.
4. Know that when you're angry, you're not yourself. *The angry you is not the real you.* You have a lot more inner-strength than this lashing-out response.
5. Know that you have the power to keep from hurting people you love even though you feel hurt.
6. Take a time-out (leave the room or the house).
7. If anyone in the family is afraid of violence, call the police.
8. If violence is not a threat, but you are hurting each other emotionally, call (contact #):

Figure 7.5

Homework Assignment # 1

Even mild anger arousal produces major physiological changes. Most of the time these occur before conscious awareness of anger. The sooner in the arousal cycle that you acknowledge your anger, the easier it is to regulate. So it is crucial that we become aware of the effects of anger on different parts of the body.

Write what anger feels like in your:

head

eyes

mouth

cheeks

neck

shoulders/arms/hands

chest

stomach

back

Worksheet 7.6

Homework Assignment # 2

Please list your personal goals for this treatment.

Please list what will you need to do to accomplish your goals.

How will you know that you're achieving your goals? What changes will you notice in yourself?

In how you feel?

In how you behave?

Worksheet 7.7

The Power of Goals

People function at their highest levels when they have a limited number of long-term, intermediate, and short-term goals, as well as one or two primary, overriding goals.

Long-term goals for treatment—satisfying, nonconflictive relationships

It becomes much easier to meet long-term goals if we have viable intermediate goals to provide reinforcement along the way to long-term goals.

Intermediate goals—develop skills in:

self-regulation
building self-esteem
developing internal power
empowering yourself and your loved ones
building skills in attachment relationships

It becomes much easier to meet intermediate goals if we have viable short-term goals to provide reinforcement along the way.

SHORT-TERM GOALS:

1. learn at least one thing from every sentence of every handout
2. reward yourself for every single thing you learn
3. recognize the power of knowledge

Our Primary, Overriding Goal (Say aloud at least once):

I will heal my hurt, which means understanding my own deeper feelings and those of my spouse, children, and parents. I will not hurt their feelings, even if they hurt me.

Worksheet 7.8

Awareness of Internal Experience: Beliefs, Feelings, Motivations Equals Genuine Power

Awareness of thoughts, beliefs, feelings, and motivations, puts you in control of them, rather than being controlled by them.

If you are not aware of feelings, or are unable to change the ones you don't want, they will seem to "sneak up on you" and make you a *reactaholic.* Then you're like a puppet on a string that other people pull, or a robot whose buttons other people push.

Self-Ignorance is powerlessness. *Self-Knowledge* (awareness of your internal experience) is *genuine power.*

ANGER AROUSAL, BASED ON IGNORANCE OF TRUE FEELINGS, EQUALS FALSE POWER

Worksheet 7.9

The False Power of Anger Arousal

The *anger arousal cycle* does not exclusively apply to heightened anger and rage. The more subtle forms of anger also involve health-destroying arousal but are much *easier* to regulate.

The false power of anger lasts only as long as the arousal lasts, and then you feel much worse.

Self-Awareness** is the key to **genuine power.

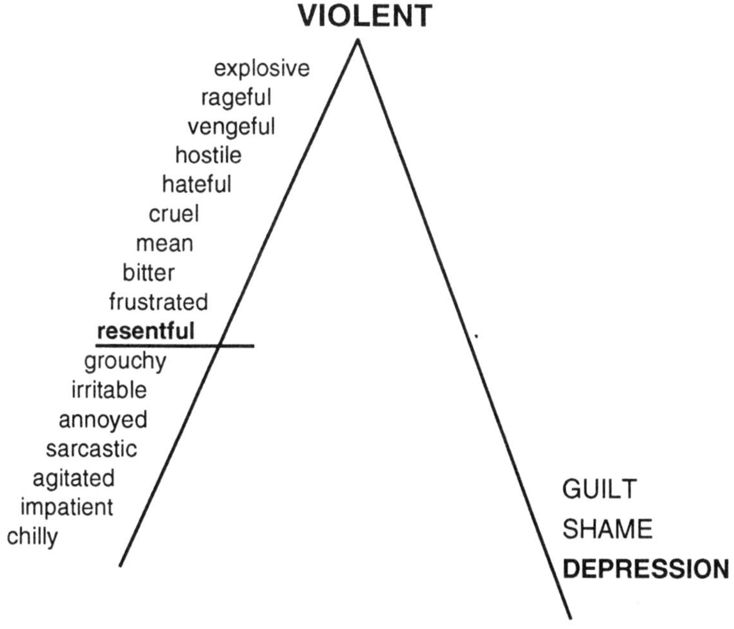

Worksheet 7.10

The Anger-Arousal Cycle: Physiological Component

(What anger does to your *body*.)

Anger comes from a small region of the brain called the limbic system. Because we share this region with all mammals, it is known as the *mammalian brain.* Anger is part of the survival-based *fight or flight* instinct we share with all mammals. The function of anger is to *mobilize* the organism for *fighting.* Hence anger is the only emotion that activates every muscle group and every organ of the body.

The chemicals secreted in the brain during anger arousal—epinephrine and norepinephrine—are experienced much like an amphetamine and analgesic—they *numb pain* and produce *a surge of energy.* That's how:

- athletes can play with broken bones and not even know about it, if they play angry
- wounded animals can be so ferocious

Massive doses of epinephrine and norepinephrine are secreted during anger arousal stimulated by the experience of physical or psychological pain or a perceived threat of physical or psychological pain. In the experience of anger:

1. The sympathetic nervous system is activated—*nerves are on edge.*
2. The heart rate accelerates.
3. Blood pressure elevates; blood surges into all muscles.
4. Eyes dilate.
5. Digestion halts (food in the stomach is either thrown-up or blasted with heavy doses of acid to process it in a hurry, which is experienced as a *burning in the stomach*); the body prepares to fight without the burden of a full stomach.

6. Messages of physical pain are blocked, so we can fight despite injuries.
7. The throat is stimulated, the voice resonates, producing an urge to roar or scream.
8. A surge of energy is produced throughout the body.

As with any amphetamine, once the surge of anger burns out, you *crash.* The experience of anger is always followed, to some degree, by depression.

Think about it: The last time you got really angry, you got really depressed afterwards. The angrier you get, the more depressed you get. And that is merely the physiological response that occurs, even if you keep from doing something while angry that you're ashamed of, like hurting the feelings of someone you love.

An *addictive* trap happens when you use anger to escape depressive mood. You may be an *anger junkie* if you use anger:

1. for energy or motivation (can't get going or keep going without some degree of anger);
2. pain-relief (it hurts when you're not angry);
3. confidence, a stronger sense of self—you only feel certain when angry;
4. to avoid depression.

The stress of anger: An arousal system meant for short bursts of ferocious energy is now evoked for prolonged bouts with unpleasant events in daily interactions.

The anger levels usually present in conflictive relationships give you a five times greater chance of dying before age 50.

High levels of anger are related to:

- destruction of T-Cells (depressing the immune system)—if you're angry a lot you probably have lots of little aches and pains, get a lot of colds and bouts of flu

- hypertension—increased threat of stroke
- heart disease
- cancer
- shortened life span

COGNITIVE (THOUGHT) COMPONENT

A great many studies confirm the old saw about being so mad you can't think straight. All thought processes are severely impaired during anger arousal. This includes:

thoughts and judgment
reality-testing (That's why sometimes after being angry you have to ask someone, "Did that really happen? Did she say that? Did he do that?"
perception (hearing or seeing things inaccurately)
learning and memory (We can't learn new things, can only remember things that happen at times when angry. That's why, when angry, you can remember a fight with a spouse or the disrespect of a child that happened years ago, but can't remember any of the sweet and pleasant things they have done since.)
problem-solving (Don't even try to solve a problem when angry.)
creativity (The only thing the brain can do is find creative reasons to stay angry.)
performance competence (With the lone exception of hurting someone, *anything* you can do angry, you can do *better* not angry.

When angry, we *misread social cues* and mistakenly assume that others are angry and hostile at us.

Anger *polarizes* thoughts—you take a more extreme position than you really believe. This makes it difficult to reach any kind of compromise.

Anger causes *thought contraction*, a drastic narrowing of the range of thoughts, so that the person whom you normally love and care about now seems like nothing other than a devil who must be hurt.

Anger is an attribution of *blame*—"I feel bad and it's your fault!" The more you blame, the angrier you get; blame makes you powerless.

Thoughts and language come from the *cerebral cortex*, unique to humans. It's the *human* part of the brain, as opposed to the *animal* part where anger originates.

The cerebral cortex is not fully developed until age 25, whereas the capacity for anger arousal is developed at age 5. Anger comes from the *child's* brain, thoughts come from the *adult* brain.

In this treatment you will learn to use the *adult* brain to regulate the *child's* brain, the *human* brain to regulate the *animal* brain.

BEHAVIORAL COMPONENT

The goal of all behavior during anger arousal is to ward-off the perceived potential attacker with aggression. This may be accomplished with attempts to:

- control-neutralize
- warn-threaten-intimidate (cats arch their backs, bulls kick sand, dogs show their teeth, humans become tense, rigid, and ready to spring)
- inflict injury on the feelings or body

When angrily arguing about bills, you don't just want to make a point, you want to control your spouse's decision, make him or her back-off, or feel stupid or inferior for not agreeing with you. *These are the sole functions of anger.*

PSYCHOLOGICAL COMPONENT

In an environment in which humankind has long since prevailed over the saber-toothed tiger, wooly mammoth, and other nightmarish predators, the principal function of anger is to protect us from psychic pain. The primary purpose of anger is to numb the pain of these feelings:

- *disregarded*
- *unimportant*
- *accused (guilty, untrustworthy, or distrusted)*
- *devalued*
- *rejected*
- *powerless*
- *unlovable*
- *unfit for human contact*

We call these feelings "*core hurts.*" Three things about core hurts are important. They constitute:

1. injuries to the sense of self and to self-esteem
2. injuries to the attachment bond (emotional ties to children, lovers, parents)
3. the most severe, non-traumatic psychic pain.

Anger provides an immediate surge of energy and numbing of pain—a feeling of *power*—to replace the powerlessness of the core hurts. So if anger works, you're *not aware* that you're feeling the core hurts—it's the *job* of anger to *numb* pain, so you can attack those whom you perceive to be causing the pain.

1. While anger numbs the pain of the core hurts, it *prevents* them from *healing.* Anger functions like *ice on a wound.* As long as you hold ice on a wound, you won't feel pain, but neither will the wound heal, and the pain will come crashing back when the ice is removed.
2. Anger makes you more sensitive to core feelings, so that you have to stay angry all the time to protect your-

self from the pain. It gives you a low tolerance of and sensitivity to pain. This tends to make you:

- easily insulted
- get furious at any kind of criticism
- always *have* to be "right"
- demand entitlements and special consideration (The world owes you a living!)
- difficult to get along with at work and home.

3. Because it focuses attention outside yourself, anger makes you *powerless* to regulate *internal* experience.

Anger alienates you from your true internal experience, your true thoughts, beliefs, and feelings. Like a drug high, maintaining anger arousal is the only important thing.

This is why the *angry* you is the *not* the *real* you.

Worksheet 7.11

Genuine Power: Compassion

Anger and aggression are not genuine power, but merely *temporary destructive arousal states*, which we sometimes *confuse* with power.

Genuine power entails a degree of control, self-awareness, and awareness of others that is impossible during anger arousal.

When turned on intimates, anger *always* resolves in some degree of guilt, shame, abandonment anxiety, and depression. Compassion, on the other hand, provides the genuine emotional power of well-being. *You can do something out of compassion, think about it 10 years later and feel good about yourself. And you can do something to a loved one out of anger, think about it 10 years later and feel bad about yourself.* Compassion replaces an illusion of power with genuine power.

COMPASSION AND HEALING

Our innate capacity for self-compassion and compassion for others *heals* the hurt that gives rise to anger and aggression, while providing genuine personal power, security, well-being, and self-esteem.

Worksheet 7.12

Self-Compassion

Self-compassion *(seeing beneath our own defenses and symptoms)* sustains compassion for others. We must understand and validate what we feel ourselves before we can understand and validate the feelings of others.

The three steps of self-compassion are necessary for healing, well-being, self-esteem, personal power, genuine pride, trust, and nondependent love:

1. understanding the true internal experience of self (what anger, anxiety, numbness, manipulation, and depression conceal);
2. validation of true feelings;
3. *changing the meaning* that causes hurtful feelings.

COMPASSION FOR OTHERS, ESPECIALLY LOVED ONES

Compassion for others *(seeing beneath their defenses and symptoms)* sustains self-compassion. We have to understand and feel for other people, especially loved ones, to fully understand and feel for ourselves.

The steps of compassion for others:

1. understanding the true internal experience of others (what anger, anxiety, depression, manipulation, and emotional withdrawal conceals);
2. validation of true feelings;
3. giving support as *they* change the meaning that causes hurtful feelings.

Worksheet 7.13

Shadows of the Heart

There's a problem with the healing power of compassion: It gets turned off by failure to stop hurt. The more you've been hurt, the harder it is to feel compassion.

If you've been hurt a lot, you may have to *reactivate* compassion, through a deeper understanding. This is an understanding so deep that you couldn't do it as a child, you can only do it as an adult, with fully developed reasoning power.

To help make a bridge from childhood hurt to full adult power, we're going to take advantage of perhaps the most powerful of adult instincts: To rescue a child in danger.

The video you're going to see depicts a child in psychological danger. He sees his mother abused. Like all young children, he blames himself for the abuse. As you're watching, *focus on the child*, and see what you feel for him. Think of how you could help him.

Worksheet 7.14

Homework Assignment # 3

QUESTIONS ABOUT *SHADOWS OF THE HEART*

1. List what the child in the video felt during and after the violence:

2. What did *you* feel for the child? Did you want to protect him? Did you want to understand and validate his feelings? If so, your response is called *compassion.*

3. How does your reaction to the child compare to anger? Which feeling do you prefer? Which makes you feel more whole, gives a more solid sense of self?

4. What kind of effect does witnessing violence have on children?

5. Will it be easy for this child to grow up liking himself or feeling proud of himself?

6. If this were your child, how could you help him with the anger that will give him the impulse to hurt other people when he feels hurt?

7. What was the mother feeling? (Why did she say such a hurtful thing to the child—did she not care about him?)

8. **What kind of effect does violence have on a woman? (Will it be easy for her to like herself or feel proud of herself?)**

9. **Is she likely to be defensive or aggressive in reaction? (Is she likely to hurt back any way she can?)**

10. **What was the father feeling?**

11. How did he numb his pain (after taking the child from the mother)?

12. **What else might he have done to numb the pain?**

So here's the vicious cycle. The father feels shame, uses anger to numb his pain, does something in anger that produces greater shame.

The mother feels shame, uses anger to numb the pain, does something that produces greater shame.

The child doesn't have anybody to hurt, he has to grow up to hurt somebody. It's relentless; we almost always do something in anger that causes greater shame.

13. **What about the man who was ordered into treatment? Could you see where his anger was coming from?**

14. **How did his anger *look*?**

15. **How does *your* anger look?**

16. **How does your anger look to your spouse?**

17. **To your children?**

Worksheet 7.15

Compassion/Assertiveness Arousal

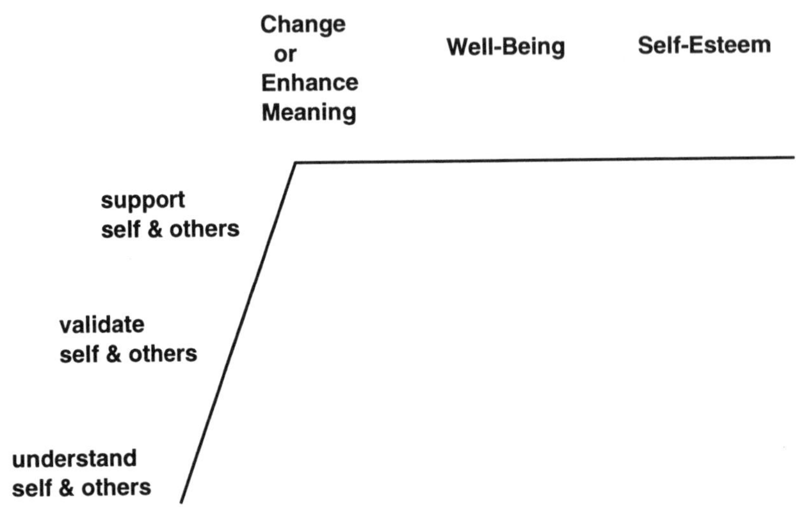

Worksheet 7.16

The Golden Rule of Internal Power

Don't turn to loved ones to regulate defenses or symptoms such as anger, anxiety, depression, or obsessions, even if you believe that they caused the symptoms.

Although you have been hurt by loved ones, defenses and symptoms are caused by the hurtful *meaning* about the *self* that *you* give to external events, including the behavior of loved ones. *Only you* can change that meaning with *self-compassion.* (Once you have done so, you can request reasonable changes in any behavior that creates problems for the family. And, of course, *all* abusive behavior must stop immediately.)

When we expect loved ones to change our internal experience, we suffer *emotional dependency.* This creates enormous **resentment** and **bitterness** in both parties. The dependent person forfeits the basic human need for personal power (the ability to control one's own thoughts, feelings, and behavior), and holds his or her loss of personal power against the person depended on, whereas the person depended on feels taken advantage of and smothered, and holds that against the dependent person.

Our performance in close relationships must be like that of musicians in orchestras and bands. Each person plays his or her own instrument competently. Each can make wonderful music on his or her own. But together, they can make something greater than any one of them can do alone: *harmony.* In harmony, they support one another to bring out the best in one another. However, harmony can't work if one member depends on the other to play his or her instrument. *We each have to play our own instruments in life, regulate our own emotions, heal our own hurts, and find partners who will not interfere with our right and responsibility to do these things.*

Worksheet 7.17

Learning the New Emotional-Regulation Skill (*H*EALS) Based on Self-Compassion and Compassion for Loved Ones

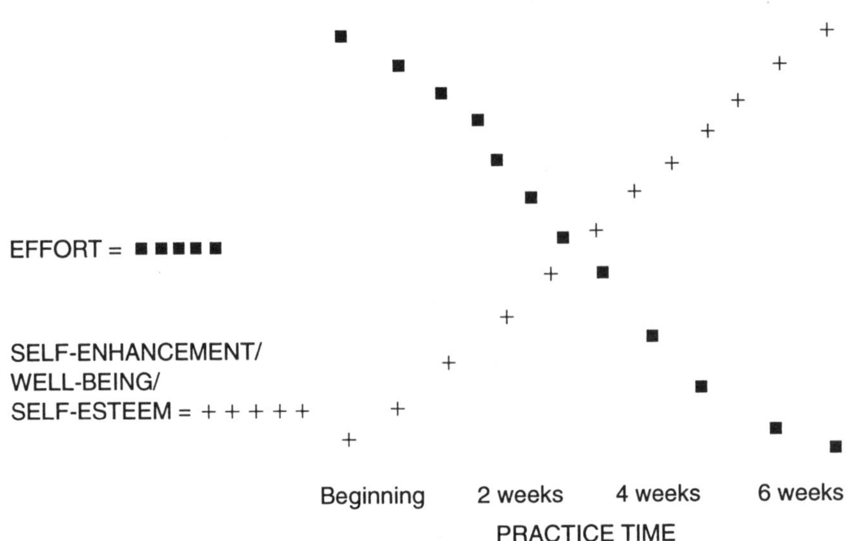

Worksheet 7.18

*H*EALS: Exercise, Skill, Vaccination

The emotion-regulation technique, *H*EALS, functions in three ways.

1. *H*EALS works like an *exercise*, like push-ups. How often and how much do you have to do it? *Until it's easy and automatic.*

   Just as the number of push-ups required to get in shape and stay in shape varies with each individual, so does the number of times you have to do the steps of *H*EALS.

   But however much time you spend practicing *H*EALS, it will only be a *tiny fraction* of the time you spend being angry, irritable, bitter, frustrated, grouchy, annoyed, impatient, anxious, and depressed.

2. *H*EALS works like a *skill*, like shooting foul shots.

   Just as you have to practice shooting foul shots over and over again, until you can hit them without having to think about it, practice *H*EALS until it just *feels* right.

   *Until it's second nature to you, practice H*EALS at least *several times per day*, and *every* time you feel angry, depressed, or anxious.

3. *H*EALS works like a *vaccination*.

   When vaccinated against a disease, very small doses of the disease are injected into the blood stream to stimulate the body to build immunity to the disease.

*H*EALS exposes you to very small doses of the core hurts that cause anger, anxiety, shame, and depression. It stimulates your brain to build a regulatory function to stop the pain of those feelings, and, with repetition, heal the wounds that cause them.

As a consequence, no one will be able to "push your buttons." Control and regulation of the meaning of your life is entirely within you, as you easily regulate the meaning that causes your painful and negative feelings.

Worksheet 7.19

HEALS

H *ealing*
E xplain to yourself
A pply self-compassion
L ove yourself
S olve

1. See the letters flash in bright colors: *HEALING*
2. Explain to yourself which is the *lowest* of the core feelings you're covering up:

    - disregarded/unimportant
    - accused: guilty or mistrusted
    - devalued
    - rejected
    - *powerless*
    - *unlovable*

    Say *slowly*, "I . . . feel . . . unlovable." *Feel* it for a few seconds.

3. **Apply self-compassion**: change the *false meaning* that hurts you (makes you angry, ashamed, guilty, depressed, obsessed, anxious)
4. Love yourself by feeling:

    COMPASSION

    - self-regard
    - important
    - **valuable**
    - *internally powerful*
    - *lovable* (compassionate)

5. Solve the problem.

Worksheet 7. 20

The Vaccination of *H*EALS

*H*EALS raises tolerance and sensitivity to the core hurts by stripping them of all negative meaning about the self. But for this step of *H*EALS to work, the core hurts must be experienced *for a few seconds.* The reason is twofold:

- We build immunity to the core hurts by developing a connection between them and higher, *healing* thought processes. With much repetition and practice over time, this connection *replaces* the connection between the core hurts and anger, anxiety, guilt, shame, obsessions, and depression. In other words, we *outgrow* them. *(Note that it will take much practice to replace the connection between the core hurts and anger/anxiety, for that has been activated for most of your life.)*
- Feeling, just for a few seconds, what the core hurts are really like, will make it clear to you that the meaning you give to the behavior of another person or to an event outside yourself is *false. Nothing* can mean that you are unimportant, unworthy of regard, unacceptable, without value, and unlovable. As you heal these feelings (by rejecting false meaning about yourself), you will no longer need anger, anxiety, and obsessions to avoid them.

Directions for feeling each core hurt in the "Explain to Yourself" step of *H*EALS.

Disregarded: Feel what it's like to feel unworthy of regard, to not count enough for anyone to pay attention to your opinions, desires, and feelings.

Unimportant: Feel what it's like to be totally unimportant, to not matter at all, to be so unimportant that no one should consider having a passing positive thought about you.

Accused/Guilty: Feel what it's like to have done something wrong, to have hurt someone, to have done terrible damage, to have betrayed someone, to have been immoral. *Accused/ Untrustworthy:* Feel what it's like to be unworthy of trust. No one can or should trust you. You are incapable of being trusted. *Accused/Distrusted:* Feel what it's like to be accused and distrusted. No matter how well you do, how innocent you are, how moral you are, you will not be trusted.

Devalued: Feel what it's like to be totally without value as a person. You are worthless.

Rejected: Feel what it's like to be completely unacceptable, to be banished, to be put down, thrown out, and abandoned.

Powerless: Feel what it's like to be completely without power over your internal experience, to be out of control of your thoughts, your feelings, and your behavior. You're like a puppet on a string or a robot whose buttons anyone can push. Anybody can make you think, feel, and do anything they want.

Unlovable: Feel what it's like to be unworthy of love. No one could love you. No one could love the real you. No one ever will.

Each of these feelings brings intense pain. They must be immediately relieved by the healing properties of *self-compassion.* With the application of self-compassion, you deeply understand that the behavior of another person or the occurrence of any event outside yourself can have no valid meaning about the self. You *are* worthy of regard, important, above accusation, valuable, acceptable, powerful, and lovable. Your compassion for others will prove it to you.

HOW AND WHERE TO PRACTICE *H*EALS

To begin with, practice on relatively mild arousal events and work up to the hard ones.

Carry your copy of the steps of *H*EALS everywhere you go.

One good place to practice *H*EALS is in front of the mirror. Observe your eyes, the color and muscle tone in your face.

Another good place to practice is in the car. Many people put the steps of *H*EALS on a small card and keep a copy in their visor.

Waiting in line or in a waiting room is a good time to practice. *There are no bad times or places to practice* H*EALS*.

The idea in practicing *H*EALS is to build a skill that will work under stress. To practice, try to recall a time when you were aroused with anger, anxiety, or obsessions. Try to locate the feeling in your body: in your eyes, face, neck, shoulders, arms, chest, stomach, and back. Try to inflame the feeling to get the level of arousal up as high as you can before working *H*EALS.

Worksheet 7.21

Weekly Log 1

- I have rehearsed *H*EALS _____ times this week (minimum 50 times).

- The steps of *H*EALS are:

- Number of times this week I successfully used *H*EALS to avoid hurting the feelings of a loved one _____.
- Number of times *H*EALS was unsuccessful (I tried it but didn't calm down) _____
- I hurt the feelings of my significant other or children this week _____ (Yes/No).
  If no, congratulate yourself! If yes, how many times? _____
- I hurt the body of my significant other or children this week _____ (Yes/No).
  If no, congratulate yourself! If yes, how many times? _____

Worksheet 7.22

Scale of Internal Power 1

As your sense of *internal power* increases, you should notice a marked reduction in items 1–8, and a marked increase in item 9.

Rate yourself on each item with the following scale:

4 = a lot
3 = some
2 = hardly at all
1 = not at all.

This week, I felt:

1. irritable. ____
2. grouchy. ____
3. annoyed. ____
4. impatient. ____
5. restless. ____
6. angry in traffic. ____
7. like there was only one "right" way to do things. ____
8. like getting revenge. ____
9. This week I felt the power to regulate anger, anxiety, obsessions, depression, manipulation (the urge to exert power and control over others). *(NOTE:* "Regulation" does not mean "avoiding" or "not thinking about it." Regulation means *changing* the *symptom.)* ____

8 The Compassion Workshop, Module Two: Dramatic Compassion

The nature and therapeutic function of compassion is the principal topic of this part of the treatment. Here client conceptions of the salient attachment emotion expand to include its intrapsychic healing and protective aspects. Worksheet 8.1 introduces the powerful role that compassion plays as a defense.

Though most clients readily embrace the use of compassion as a self-regulator, some will not. Initial resistance is likely to be twofold. In the first place, some clients might fear that compassion means capitulation in a power struggle. Actually, compassion *replaces* power struggles with a desire for mutual understanding. Most problems that people have with disputes within attachment relationships are not about failing to get their own way. Rather, the great frustration lies in feeling *misunderstood.* When loved ones don't understand us, we infer that they don't love us, and from this, that we're unlovable. Compassion eliminates this most harmful aspect of disagreement and thereby reduces the insistence of one or other party on getting what he or she wants beyond understanding and validation.

The second resistance to compassion comes from fear of having to admit the extent to which clients have hurt people they love. To ease this paralyzing anxiety, emphasize the priority of self-compassion. In practice, the therapeutically enhanced experience of self-compassion transforms the psychological perspective of most clients. From this loftier viewpoint, they can look down on past transgressions as functions of emotional dysregulation (a failure of compassion), from the jaws of which self-compassion has now delivered them. The effects of this realization convert the self-obsessive throes of shame into the prosocial motivation to make amends for past behavior, that is, to make oneself worthy of sustaining compassion for loved ones, and of receiving compassion from loved ones. *Whenever clients balk at compassion as a dominant context for interpersonal meaning-making, help them to invoke self-compassion, then point out how easily they can feel compassion for loved ones.*

Worksheet 8.2 draws comparisons between compassion and anger as regulators of core hurts. In most cases it will be sufficient to let clients read the handout on their own, outside of treatment sessions.

ABUSE AS A FAILURE OF COMPASSION

Worksheet 8.3 defines abuse as a failure of compassion. This characterization of emotional abuse constitutes the main target of treatment intervention, on the assumption, rising from clinical experience and tentatively supported by initial research (Stosny, 1993), that mildly abusive acts are failures of the same regulatory process as severely abusive ones. Learning to regulate internal experience that leads to mild abuse helps prevent more dangerous kinds of abuse.

If you suspect that your client might be an anger-junkie, offer the handout in Worksheet 8.4. For most clients it should be unnecessary to go over the handout during the treatment session. But for a few, the theme of anger arousal as an addiction requires greater emphasis. This seems particularly true with active or recovering substance abusers. The relationship of anger and abuse of substances, though widely discussed, needs further research (e.g., Potter-Efron & Potter-Efron, 1991). From a clinical standpoint it is easy to see how clients use anger to numb guilt, shame, and abandonment-anxiety, and then use substances to medicate the anger, either to quell its arousal, or alleviate the depression into which the exhausted anger arousal cycle deposits them. Although some therapists have created 12-Step subgroups of the Compassion Workshop to treat anger addiction, I prefer the corrective use of compassion applied directly to the core hurts that, in my view, lead us to rage, to hurt ourselves and the people we love, to drink, and to drug. Having said that, if therapists are comfortable with a greater emphasis on the anger-junkie theme than I have made, they are welcome to select any part of the Compassion Workshop that might help.

Worksheet 8.5 draws important distinctions between self-denigrating interpretations of emotions and the everyday experience of transient feelings states, such as loneliness, disappointment, sadness, and anxiety. Only when transient feelings invoke deficit-ridden constructions of self, do they portend challenge to the internal sense of self.

The interventive strategy underlying the handout owes much to the cognitive therapies of Beck (1976) and Ellis (1985). However, in the current formulation, experience of an unrelated and relatively superficial emotional state can trigger an habitual link to self-constructions. Thus transient and common feeling states take on the ominous importance of that which threatens the well-being if not the existence of the self. So it is simply not enough to say that the cognitive components of these constructions are irrational, for few of us have encountered many non-delusional clients who in some sense have not known that much. Rather, the therapy must protect the self from the "slings and arrows of *banal* fortune" by building immunity to rational as well as irrational constructions of everyday life. In other words, it might be perfectly rational to suppose that I am lonely because I'm not lovable, that is, not compassionate, and cognitive restructuring will scarcely correct that. However, through the experience of compassion, I will become lovable, and no cognitive restructuring alone will accomplish that. The motivation to change negative meaning (activated in step three of *H*EALS), is the experience of compassion, rather than a testing of the assumptions underlying distorted cognition. In other words, cognitive adjustment is the means of the intervention, but compassion is the motivation to use the means. This may seem like a subtle distinction, but it has the effect of transforming the emphasis from *deficits in thinking* to *assets in motivation*, allowing clients to build on strengths to correct weaknesses. The path to cognitive alterations seems much more accessible when feeling compassion than when feeling shame, guilt, and anger, or, worse, when feeling little of anything.

Worksheet 8.6 is another homework assignment intended to spur understanding of an attachment figure's point of view.

Two in-session quizzes (Worksheets 8.7 and 8.8) should be selected for processing if clients continue to maintain negative attitudes about gender roles or defend their habitual anger-violence response. The quizzes are powerful tools in changing attitudes without invoking massive resistance.

On the Anger-Violence Quiz, most clients answer, "father" or "mother," "husband" or "wife." The correct answer is a *child under 3.* This reframes the "manliness" of the anger-violence response as simply *childish.* Lacking the power of a mature cerebral cortex, children resort to anger and violence in desperate stabs at seizing power outside themselves. Adults, endowed with the natural ability to regulate emotions through higher cognitive processes, resort to such desperation without necessity and, most of the time, only by habit.

The correct answer for all the items on The Wimp Test, is, of course, *Wimp.* This reframes many of the characteristics our culture attributes to "manliness" as motivated by fear and insecurity. A "real man" feels all his feelings and appreciates the value of compassion. By this point in the treatment, even those who started with the most avid stereotypes should be able to answer all the questions correctly. Thus the test is a valuable way to gauge individual progress.

DRAMATIC COMPASSION

An 8-minute dramatic video, entitled, *Compassion*, models *H*EALS for clients. With professional actors, the video dramatizes how compassion for self and loved ones creates a greater sense of internal power than abusive behavior can possibly offer. The video begins with an altercation in which a man is about to beat his wife. Instead, he uses *H*EALS. The couple struggles, occasionally regressing to old, blaming behaviors, before fully embracing their new emotional regulatory skills. Clients viewing the video have no doubt of when they are more powerful.

The timing of when to show *Compassion* is important. On the one hand, there is temptation to show it early in treatment, so that everyone can see how it works under fire. However, if shown before clients have achieved any appreciable measure of skill in emotional regulation, they tend to get angry at the wife's "goading" or to find the topic of jealousy overwhelming. This sort of response is completely reversed if shown about 2 weeks after clients have learned *H*EALS. Then they are able to recognize that the couple on the video achieves all the more power by refusing to react childishly to childish provocation. (To acquire the video, call Intermedia, 1-800-553-8336.)

Notes for processing the video are available in Worksheet 8.9.

Worksheet 8.10 contains two more homework assignments meant to expand the capacity for compassion that enhances the attachment bond.

Worksheet 8.1

The Functions of Compassion

1. *Compassion:*

- reinforces the sense of importance, value, internal power, lovability in *both* the self and loved ones;
- builds self-esteem in *both* the self and loved ones.

Thus parents are self-enhanced as they enhance the selves of their children. Lovers are empowered as they empower one another.
2. *Compassion heals* hurt within the self and helps loved ones heal hurt within themselves.
3. *Compassion* makes us viable attachment figures, that is, *lovable.*
4. *Compassion* enhances the attachment bond that holds us in love relationships.
5. *Compassion* regulates emotions that damage the attachment bond, such as anger and fear of intimacy.

COMPASSION AS *DEFENSE*

Compassion serves two powerful *defensive* functions:

- through perspective-taking, compassion changes false meanings about the self stimulated by the behavior of others.

  Example one:
  When there is inappropriate or hurtful behavior, compassion keeps the focus on the person behaving inappropriately or causing the hurt. Thus abuse is *not internalized* as a problems of the self, but seen as *that* person's problem.

Example two:

Seeming rejection by another is *not seen* as rejection of the self but as an expression of that person's preferences, limitations, performance under stress, or, most often in attachment relationships, a *symptom of hurt.*

- Compassion rarely stimulates anger in others, making hostile or destructive defenses *unnecessary.*

COMPASSION AND DISAGREEMENT

Compassion requires validation of, and sympathy with, the feelings of another, *regardless* of disagreement about the thoughts/beliefs/ideas that go with the feelings. In other words, you can disagree 24–7 and still have compassion for one another.

Example one:

A couple disagrees about whether to have another child.

Both spouses need to make a *sincere* effort to understand the importance of the other's beliefs, goals, and desires *and* to sympathize with the desire, or the disappointment, if the desire cannot be fulfilled.

The worse thing they can do is attack or criticize or put down one another for their beliefs, goals, and desires.

Example two:

Your children do not receive this compassion training, so they do not know how to value and sympathize with feelings that result from ideas with which they disagree. *They need you to model it for them, to teach them compassion.*

Example Three:

Your parents do not receive this compassion training. Although this will make the process harder, if you use compassion, you will *enjoy* its *internal* benefits, while modeling a better way of interacting with loved ones. *Compassion tends to stimulate compassion in loved ones, almost as surely as anger stimulates anger.*

If you feel devalued by something your spouse or child or parent says or does, he or she probably said or did it out of a personal feeling of diminished value. Devaluing him or her in return will only make it *worse.* Compassion will only make it *better.*

COMPASSION VERSUS "GIVING-IN"

"Giving-in" or "going along to avoid an argument" virtually guarantees resentment. Resentment undermines and eventually ruins attachment relationships.

Most of the time resolution without resentment is possible when a sincere effort is made to understand one another. Compassion is *not* resolution, but it is *necessary* for resolution once feelings have been hurt.

Example:

Not getting this new boat or that new wardrobe does not mean that you don't deserve it. You *do* deserve it, and I'm sorry that you're disappointed that we can't get it for you. This is why we can't get it. . . .

Understanding brings the parties of a dispute closer, while anger drives them further apart. Most of the time we become the angriest (the most hurt), not when disappointed for not getting what we want, but when feeling *misunderstood* or *disregarded* or when disappointment takes on the *false* meaning that we're unimportant or unlovable. With compassion, we *never* feel unimportant or disregarded or unlovable (although we may feel disappointed). This makes negotiation on all issues much easier.

Compassion does not necessarily include generosity or magnanimity. It requires that we understand and regard the feelings of others as *vital factors*, but not the *only factors*, in decisions.

We can never feel taken advantage of or exploited in the experience of compassion, for compassion is its own reward. Even if it turns out that we were manipulated by someone else's defenses or weaknesses, we have the self-satisfaction of knowing that we acted out of compassion, which is always the right thing.

With compassion we avoid the leading cause of death of attachment relationships: *Power Struggles.* With compassion the goal is not to "win" a dispute, but to find a solution in which *all* parties feel regarded, important, and valuable.

COMPASSION MEANS *NOT* TOLERATING ABUSE

Compassion helps us explain and forgive unacceptable behavior, but also requires that unacceptable behavior change *and* that abusive behavior *stop immediately*, for the sake of everyone in the family.

Compassion relieves blame, but at the same time, *increases responsibility.*

- No one is to blame for being hurt or damaged. But each person is responsible for healing the hurt and repairing the damage before they drive him or her to hurt others.

Worksheet 8.2

Self-Regulation: Compassion v. Anger

Compassion	**Anger**
heals self and loved ones	hurts self and loved ones
regulates and *heals* core feelings	hides core hurts, *prevents* healing
you control it	you're out of control
no blame—anger response seen as a symptom of hurt, not evil intention	blame—blame—blame
builds power within	makes you a powerless victim
refutes accusations	confirms accusations
think much more clearly; uses adult brain	thought processes severely impaired, use child's brain
creates well-being	ends in depression
do things you are proud of	do things you're ashamed of
converts shame into pride	converts pride into shame
allows negotiation on the *issue*	can only be about feelings
a genuine compassionate response calms anger in others	inflames the anger of everyone around you

independent of the response of others	totally dependent on the response of others
works as a: 1. pain-reliever 2. confidence-builder—stronger sense of self 3. energizer and motivator	works as a: 1. pain-reliever 2. confidence-builder—stronger sense of self 3. energizer and motivator

Worksheet 8.3

Failures of Compassion: Definitions of Abuse

Abuse is hurting the feelings or the body of someone else to alter some unpleasant feeling within yourself. Because compassion regulates unpleasant internal feelings, all abuse is a *failure of compassion.*

Physical abuse:

hitting, punching, slapping, pushing, grabbing, kicking, and any unwanted touching, sexual or non-sexual, as well as threatening, coercing, or intimidating.

Emotional abuse:

an attack on a person's autonomy, identity, privacy, sense of self, or self-esteem—attempting to control, isolate, or force behavior against his or her will

attacking or criticizing what a person *is*, rather than what she or he does.

Abusive	**Nonabusive**
"You're lazy."	"I feel you can do a little more to help keep the house clean."
"You're stupid."	"I disagree with your opinion."
"You're a slut."	"I felt jealous when I saw you talking to him. I need to regulate my jealousy."

"You're a bitch."	"I feel bad when you shout like that."
"You're a bad kid."	"I don't like it when you talk disrespectfully to me."

Does hurting the feelings of a loved one ever *stop* him or her from hurting yours? Does hurting a loved one ever solve the problem, or does it create more problems (such as continual resentment and hostility)?

Worksheet 8.4

The Anger-Junkie's Constant Song: "Justifying the Anger Blues"

The most destructive and dangerous of emotions, anger is also the most socially inhibited; the gravest laws are designed to stop anger-driven behavior.

In general, anger is socially acceptable only when mitigating circumstances justify it. Hence, the anger-addicted brain, in need of epinephrine and norepinephrine for energy and relief of pain, constantly seeks *justification* of anger, *ignoring all contrary evidence* in the process.

When the brain needs a jolt of epinephrine and norepinephrine, judgment and reasoning are greatly impaired. *Failure to comprehend most relevant possibilities is virtually guaranteed* in the lust to see only those possibilities that justify anger. That's why anger-junkies justifying their anger sound like alcoholics trying to justify their drinking by suggesting that alcohol has nutritional value.

Regardless of personal levels of intelligence, *during anger arousal* we perform generally as if we have a *thought disorder or learning disability.* The most common thought distortions that occur during anger arousal:

- construing the self as victim—blaming others for your internal experience
- all-or-nothing thinking (no shades of gray)
- polarized thinking—taking a position more extreme or even contrary to actual beliefs
- ego-centralizing—can see no one else's point of view
- catastrophizing—this is terrible, no matter how trivial
- over-generalizing—if everybody did the trivial thing, the world would be horrible; or this *always* happens, you *always* do that, you *never* do this

- paranoia—everyone's trying to make you feel bad
- mental processing errors:

  - misreading social cues—supposing that others feel the same way you do
  - visual processing—don't see what's actually there, or see things that aren't actually there
  - auditory processing—can't hear what is actually said or imagine you hear something different
  - reading processing—misunderstanding what is read
  - emotional numbing—out of touch with all emotions or with all emotions except anger

Except for warning, intimidating, or inflicting verbal, emotional, and physical injury, everything you can do angry, *you can do better not angry.*

General Rule:

> **If you have to justify your emotions or behavior, to yourself or others, they are almost always *harmful.***

The urge to justify should be a trigger to *heal the hurt that causes the anger.* Justifying anger will *never* heal the hurt that causes it.

Are You an Anger-Junkie?

You may be an *anger junkie* if you use anger:

1. for energy or motivation (can't get going or keep going without some degree of anger);
2. for pain-relief (it hurts when you're not angry);
3. for confidence, a stronger sense of self—you only feel certain when angry;
4. to avoid depression;
5. to enforce a sense of entitlement;
6. to inhibit or punish disagreement with your opinions and values;

7. more than once a day, and when you experience anger, it lasts for more than a few minutes.

The cure for anger addiction is compassion for self and loved ones.

Worksheet 8.5

Normal Feelings versus Defenses and Symptoms

The difference between the experience of healthy negative feelings and that of symptoms and defenses is the *meaning about the self* that we give to the experience. For example, the following are common, *everyday* feelings.

- disappointment
- sadness
- loneliness
- anxiety
- distress/upset

Only when *disappointment, sadness, loneliness, anxiety, and distress/upset* seem to *mean* something about the self, do they stimulate defenses and symptoms of anger, anxiety, obsessions, or depression.

If disappointment *means* that I'm unimportant, unregardable, not valuable, rejectable, unlovable, then it stimulates defenses and symptoms.

If sadness *means* that I'm unimportant, unregardable, not valuable, etc., it stimulates defenses and symptoms.

If loneliness *means* that I'm defective, inadequate, incomplete, unimportant, unlovable, etc., it stimulates defenses and symptoms.

If anxiety *means* that I'm unimportant, unregardable, not valuable, etc., it stimulates defenses and symptoms.

If distress *means* that I'm unimportant, unregardable, not valuable, etc., it stimulates defenses and symptoms.

HOW BAD FEELINGS GET WORSE

Disappointment = She doesn't care about me = I'm not lovable.

Sadness = Nobody loves or understands me.

Loneliness = I can't function when I'm alone or jealous. (I'm not loveable, so he or she must want someone else.)

Anxiety = Something bad will happen and I will be powerless to control my feelings.

Distress/upset = I feel bad and somebody is to blame! Somebody else has to fix it!

THE CURE: SELF-COMPASSION

Disappointment, sadness, loneliness, anxiety, and *distress/upset* are common human experiences; they mean nothing about the self. We need to learn to experience these common feelings without allowing them to contaminate the self. They're no big deal; we can handle them!

Homework Assignment # 4

NORMAL FEELINGS V. DEFENSES AND SYMPTOMS EXERCISE

Write an example for each of the following. How to keep:

loneliness from becoming jealousy, abandonment, unlovability;

("Not thinking about it" or "ignoring it" won't work. You need to *regulate* the feelings through self-enhancement, that is, "I *am* worthy of love; my loneliness just means that I'm lonely, not that I'm unlovable.")

disappointment from becoming rejection;

sadness from becoming unlovability;

anxiety from becoming loss of control;

distress/upset from becoming blame.

Worksheet 8.6

Homework Assignment # 5
Understanding One Another

In the space below, write, in as much detail as possible, the point of view of your spouse/significant other, parents, or children in your last argument.

What was he or she thinking?

What was she or he feeling?

Did he or she feel that you understood him or her?

How would she (he) describe you at that moment (what did your behavior seem like to her or him?)

Did you feel understood by him (her)?

What might you have done to make yourself better understood?

Worksheet 8.7

The Anger-Violence Quiz

Please identify the family member to whom the question most likely refers.

1. **Who are the most violent people in the vast majority of families?**

2. **This family member most often uses anger as a defense.**

3. **If this family member doesn't get his/her own way, violence is likely.**

4. **If hurt or offended, this family member wants to hit or throw something.**

5. **This family member has fits of temper.**

Worksheet 8.8

The Wimp Test

Put an *M* next to those statements you think describe a *real man*, or a *W*, next to those statements you think describe a *wimp*.

1. He's afraid to be honest.
2. He won't admit to himself what he really feels.
3. He's afraid to take responsibility for himself and blames others for what he thinks, feels, and does.
4. He's afraid to feel like an adult and give up the defenses of a two year-old.
5. He's afraid to internalize power, and instead relies on other people to make him feel powerful and to make him feel good or bad.
6. He can't feel good about himself unless he feels better than someone else.
7. He's afraid to be intimate.
8. He's afraid to be compassionate.
9. He hides behind anger, because:
   a. He's afraid to feel disregarded and unimportant.
   b. He's afraid to feel devalued.
   c. He's afraid to feel rejected.
   d. He's afraid to feel unlovable.
10. Is a real man *afraid* to feel hurt? Does he *need* to cover up his feelings with anger and violence?
11. Would a real man hurt a woman or a child to keep from feeling a few seconds of rejection, or disrespect, or devaluation?

Worksheet 8.9

The Video, *Compassion*

1. When was he more powerful?
    a. When accusing?
    or
    b. When understanding?
2. When was he more powerful?
    a. When blaming her for his feelings?
    or
    b. When taking responsibility for them?
3. When was he more powerful?
    a. When angry
    or
    b. When compassionate?
4. When he saw her talk to someone at a party, what did his perception of her behavior mean to him about himself?

5. After regulating his own hurt, what did that same behavior—her talking to someone at a party—mean to him?

Worksheet 8.10

Homework Assignment # 6
Supporting the Attachment Bond

Whether we like it or not, a bond forms between people in attachment relationships. The attachment bond can be either attacked and resented, or enhanced and supported.

List at least five things you can do to enhance and support your attachment bond with your spouse/significant other.

List at least five things you can do to enhance and support your attachment bond with your children or parents.

Homework Assignment # 7

COMPASSION MEANS:

1. Seeing beneath defenses and symptoms (such as anger, anxiety, depression, emotional withdrawal), to understand the core hurts causing defenses and symptoms.

2. Validating the core-feelings causing the defenses or symptoms.

3. Changing the meaning of the *validated* feelings.

List the reasons to feel compassion (to understand, sympathize and support) for:

Your spouse/significant other

1.
2.
3.
4.
5.
6.
7.
8.
9.
10.

Your children or parents:

1.
2.
3.
4.

5.
6.
7.
8.
9.
10.

Yourself:

1.
2.
3.
4.
5.
6.
7.
8.
9.
10.

9 The Compassion Workshop, Module Three: Self-Enpowerment; Module Four: Empowerment of Loved Ones

MODULE THREE: SELF-EMPOWERMENT THROUGH LATERAL SELF-ESTEEM

This part of the treatment demonstrates that clients cannot feel good about themselves so long as they suppress compassion for those they love. Due to the self-building function of attachment relationships, hurting or diminishing attachment figures invariably hurts and diminishes the self. This realization makes possible an escape from the trap of low self-esteem into which attachment abusers continually stumble.

Worksheet 9.1 describes the elements of high and low self-esteem.

Attachment abusers often fall prey to hierarchical self-esteem, in the throes of which they need to feel better than someone else to feel good about themselves (see Worksheet 9.2). In the most virulent form of this affliction—*predatory* self-esteem—abusers, to feel assured of their own fragile sense of self, need to make others feel bad about themselves; they require the subservience of significant others to a false and sorely inadequate sense of self. When the prey is an attachment figure, the predator battles floods of guilt and shame (often blamed on the attachment figure and converted into still more anger and hostility), and falls into yet another kind of trap. The attachment abuser who needs to feel superior to a spouse or child will tend to feel ashamed of that spouse or child in public, in the belief that the world at large shares his or her distorted view of persecuted attachment figures.

Once clients have seen the reality of this self-destructive form of shallow and temporary self-enhancement, the treatment can transform self-esteem in general beyond the limits of attachment relationships. Now clients can grow from no-win hierarchical constructions, in which people are pegged "superior" or "inferior," to no-lose lateral constructions, in which everyone is equal.

LATERAL SELF-ESTEEM VERSUS DOWNWARD COMPARISON

The human capacity for what Wills (1981) calls *downward comparison* allows estimates of self-worth to be based on those worse off than us. Wills presents evidence that some people enhance their subjective well-being by comparing themselves to those less fortunate. A subtle difference between the adaptability of downward comparison (Baumeister, 1991) on the one hand, and the maladaptability of hierarchical self-esteem on the other, lies in the implicit victimization of the comparison: "Those below me *should* feel worse about themselves than I do," which implies, "I *should* feel less self-worth than those above me." In contrast, the adaptable use of downward comparison views those "below" far less insidiously, as merely less fortunate, in circumstance or in the genetic lottery or both, which implies that those "above" are merely more fortunate. Unless the object of comparison is an attachment figure, this adaptable form of downward comparison is quite similar to the concept of lateral self-esteem promoted in the Compassion Workshop.

GENUINE PRIDE AND SELF-ESTEEM

Worksheet 9.3 describes self-esteem as a kind of inner pride, morale, or spirit to accomplish something. The construct divides into genuine and false or narcissistic pride. False pride is externally regulated and sometimes based on just one or two aspects of self, but never the whole self. *Genuine* pride must include all important aspects of self: competence, growth, creativity, self-nurturance, and compassion for self and others.

Worksheet 9.4 informs clients that self-esteem is within their ability to manipulate and that systematic enhancement of self-esteem is a learnable skill. Two companion homework assignments provide important exercises and key indicators of how well clients are assimilating the treatment and of how much additional work may be necessary.

Worksheet 9.5, distinguishing blame from responsibility, describes the effects of each on self-esteem. This is a difficult distinction that clients must understand to gain control of the meaning of their experience.

The Self-Esteem Transfusion Schedule (Worksheet 9.6) is a homework assignment that must be done once a day, over 10 consecutive days. I have tested this clinical tool of self-esteem enhancement in many different ways, and in various repetitions. Once a day for 10 straight days produced the optimal boost in self-esteem. If clients should miss more than 1 day, however, it is better to start the 10-day streak over again. They will appreciate the difference the Schedule makes within a few days as they notice their scores steadily rising. (Note: Numbers 22 and 23 are skipped on the schedule. Only if these are left blank on the answer sheets can you be assured that clients are not merely rendering response sets.)

Worksheet 9.7 is a written exercise. I prefer to do it within the treatment session, and then have clients read their work aloud, to underscore the differences in their voices as they say an item on the core hurt list with its corresponding correction item. Similar exercises, Worksheets 9.8 and 9.9, can be done at home. However, the correction part of the assignments should be read aloud in the treatment session; clients cannot hear themselves too often making verbal corrections of distorted self-constructions.

Worksheet 9.10 is a homework assignment that should indicate substantial improvement in client knowledge of viable means of emotional regulation.

Worksheet 9.11 demonstrates the link between compassionate morality and self-esteem. Worksheet 9.12 introduces the Compassion Shield to reinforce the connections between self-esteem, power, self-protection, and compassion.

Worksheet 9.13 forms a link between Modules Two and Three by equating internal power (necessary for self-esteem) with interpersonal power. The Building Power Within quiz (Worksheet 9.14) can be adapted as appropriate for various attachment figures.

MODULE FOUR: THE HEART DISEASE OF FAMILIES—POWER STRUGGLES

Up to this point in the Compassion Workshop, power has been framed as a completely internal feeling. The assumption has been that people only try to exert power over others if they feel powerless over their internal experience. In Module Four, the redefinition of power takes on interpersonal significance. Here the construction of empowerment replaces client conceptions of *power over* loved ones. In their research of spouse abusers, Dutton and Strachan (1987) urge that intervention help abusers reconceptualize power as an interdependent rather than adversarial phenomenon. In that vein, Module Four of the Compassion Workshop suggests that the self is diminished whenever attachment figures are diminished, just as the self is enhanced as attachment figures are enhanced. Genuine interpersonal power, and the self-esteem derived from it, are achieved by shifting one's constructive goal from winning a dispute to finding a solution about which everyone can feel important, regarded, respected, and valuable. Thus empowerment of loved ones becomes a source of personal power.

Worksheet 9.15 describes the danger that power struggles present to attachment relationships. Worksheet 9.16 is another quiz to reframe power and to gauge client progress. Worksheets 9.17, 9.18, and 9.19 continue the reframing of power as an internal phenomenon to be enhanced through empowerment of loved ones.

Worksheet 9.1

Elements of High Self-Esteem

Research on people with high self-esteem has shown that they have the following qualities:

1. self-control (regulation of thoughts, feelings, behavior)
2. knowledge that they have competently done or will do what they sincerely believe to be the right thing
3. respect for and value of other people
4. self-reward—what they *do*, not what others think of them, is their primary reward
5. control of personal meaning (not of others or events).

A person with LOW SELF-ESTEEM:

1. blames others for his feelings and behavior (which makes him powerless)
2. hurts feelings or body of others
3. can't control emotions
4. relies on the response of others to feel good about himself
5. expects to fail and blames it on others or on the situation or some defect of the self

The Lesson:

The road to psychological *ruin* begins with *blame.*

The road to psychological *power* beings with *responsibility.*

Worksheet 9.2

Hierarchical Self-Esteem: No Way to Win

Persons with hierarchical self-esteem need to feel better than someone else to feel good about themselves. They view people in terms of *superiority* and *inferiority*. Not surprisingly, this form of self-esteem lies at the heart of racism, sexism, and all other prejudicial points of view.

Hierarchical self-esteem is a virtually unachievable goal: You will *always* meet people superior to you. You will always meet persons who are smarter, wealthier, more powerful, better looking, more popular, and so on; failure is the inevitable end of this precarious notion of self-worth.

The most abusive form of hierarchical self-esteem is *predatory self-esteem*. To feel good about themselves, persons with predatory self-esteem need to make other people feel bad about themselves. Their most frequent victims are members of their own families. Many family abusers in therapy test high in self-esteem, whereas everyone else in the family tests low. When intervention increases the self-esteem of the emotionally beaten-down spouse and children, the predator's self-esteem declines. The only successes allowed to family members are those that directly enhance the predator.

Of course, predatory self-esteem is always false self-esteem, for it rises on a rush of anger or criticism used to put down other people. When anger arousal wears off or the criticism is no longer internalized by the victims, the predator drops once again into depression, with the added burden of shame for having hurt loved ones.

LATERAL SELF-ESTEEM: THE POWER OF EQUALITY

A no-lose approach to self-esteem invokes the *power of equality*. If you believe in the essential equality of all people, you will never meet anyone better than you. A steady supply of self-esteem comes from efforts to increase other people's self-esteem, by treating them, without regard to station or status, with dignity and respect. *The royal road to self-regard and self-empowerment passes through regard and empowerment of others.*

Worksheet 9.3

Genuine Self-Esteem = Genuine Pride

Self-esteem is a form of *pride* that includes motivation to do something; it provides *morale* or the *spirit to go on.* Although this sort of motivation or morale can be activated by what other people think, it is more effective and genuine when it rises from deeply held personal values and conviction.

False Pride afflicts those with:

- hierarchical or predatory self-esteem
- exclusively external measures of self-esteem (what other people think), with no personal values or conviction base
- investment of pride in merely one or two aspects of the self, while other crucial aspects are cut off or denied or shrouded in shame and failure.

False pride requires self-obsession to maintain. Those afflicted must continually *manipulate* others to keep the illusion going. They see others only as sources of feelings or pleasure or convenience, and not separate persons in their own right. They violate their *most humane need:* to experience genuine compassion.

A person with *false pride* is so self-obsessed that he or she is either never satisfied with success (it's never enough, so long as it is isolated from the total self) or fails to recognize blatant indications of failure in work and intimate relationships. *Genuine Self-Esteem* must include genuine pride in *all* the Power Modes of self:

competence
growth/creativity

healing/nurturing
compassion.

Examples of false pride:

- The Nazis were competent and creative without being compassionate.
- Many physicians are competent, creative, and healing, without being nurturing or compassionate.
- Many people are nurturing without being competent or truly compassionate (which involves understanding).

Compassion is the most fertile wellspring of *genuine pride and genuine self-esteem*, for compassion includes each of the other Power Modes of self. *Genuine pride*, as opposed to false (or narcissistic) pride, entails pride in oneself as a *competent, creative, growth-oriented, nurturing, compassionate* person.

Worksheet 9.4

Taking Charge of Your Self-Esteem

GENERAL RULE:

- Make your primary goal—in everything you do—the enhancement of self-esteem.
- Concentrate on giving yourself continual jolts of self-esteem—of good feelings about yourself.
- The overriding questions in everything you do must be:
  What will make me feel best about myself?
  What will make me feel the most genuine pride?

REMEMBER:

- Genuine pride for human beings involves caring about someone else, feeling **COMPASSION.**
- Blame gives control of your self-esteem to someone else.
- Responsibility gives you complete control of your self-esteem.
- Reward yourself for:
  - □ every act of self-control,
  - □ every time you do the right thing,
  - □ respecting and valuing other people, whether they "deserve" it or not,
  - □ dissipating negative feelings by controlling your personal meaning.

Homework Assignment #8

FROM ANGER JUNKIE TO SELF-ESTEEM JUNKIE

List an example of something that could be damaging to your self-esteem.

List how you will convert it into a self-esteem jolt.

Why should we respect and value people "whether they deserve it or not?"

Worksheet 9.5

Blame versus Responsibility

The road to psychological ruin begins with blame.

Blame involves an attribution of immoral or negative intent (evil, recklessness, carelessness) that is almost always *inaccurate.*

Blame obscures solutions by *locking you into the problem.*

Blame makes you a *powerless* victim.

The road to psychological power begins with responsibility.

Responsibility focuses on *solutions.* Any consideration not having to do with solutions (such as fixing blame) is irrelevant.

Responsibility is power.

Example: Someone plows into my car parked legally on the street. That's not my fault. But it's my responsibility to get it fixed. As long as I *blame* the hit-and-run driver (or myself for parking there) for the expense and inconvenience of the accident, I am riddled with anger and anxiety.

But as I assume *responsibility* for the repairs I *empower* myself with transportation. In addition, I am:

- doing the right thing in the circumstance
- regulating anxiety and anger that diminish self-esteem
- giving myself a jolt of self-esteem

I *reward* myself for acting responsibly. Now getting my car is like an injection of self-esteem, rather than a blast of shame and anger. I'm pleased by how resourceful I am.

We are *not to blame* if we are hurt, but we're each *responsible to heal our own hurt.*

Homework Assignment # 9

Write about an incident in which you were able to take charge of your self-esteem.

How were you able to take charge of your self-esteem in this incident?

Write about an incident in which your self-esteem was attacked/controlled by someone else.

What could you have done differently to take charge of your self-esteem in this incident?

Worksheet 9.6

Homework Assignment # 10 The Self-Esteem Transfusion Schedule

NOTE: save these pages for future use (turn in the answer sheets only)

The Self-Esteem Transfusion Schedule does more than measure self-esteem; it gives a *boost* to the way you feel about yourself. The Schedule serves as a reminder to think, feel, and behave in ways that promote self-esteem. Completed on a daily basis, it injects small doses of self-esteem. Over time, these accumulate to a powerful sense of pride and compassion.

Low-scored items indicate areas for further work, either on your own or in therapy or support group discussion.

Answer each item as carefully and accurately as you can by placing a number beside each one as follows:

5 = strongly agree
4 = agree
3 = neutral
2 = disagree
1 = strongly disagree

1. I forgive my mistakes. ____
2. I can learn at least one thing at almost every waking moment of my life. ____
3. I know more than I knew yesterday. ____
4. I understand more than I understood yesterday. ____

5. I value my feelings. ____
6. I can feel compassion for others, without feeling overwhelmed by their misfortune. ____
7. I am honest and kind. ____
8. I am freeing myself of shame by expressing it out loud, to myself and to another person. ____
9. I treat others with respect and dignity. ____
10. I treat myself with respect and dignity. ____
11. I can love. ____
12. I am worthy of love. ____
13. Even though there may be aspects of my behavior or beliefs that I want to change, I accept myself unconditionally. ____

As I think of the following items, they are *reminders* to be kind and gentle with myself, at *this* moment:

14. I am treating myself with affection. ____
15. I am being kind to myself. ____
16. I am being gentle with myself. ____
17. I have done healthful exercise in the past 24 hours. ____
18. I have tried to resolve my conflicts with others, with fairness, compassion, and a desire to understand. ____
19. I have tried to resolve conflicts within myself, with fairness, compassion, and a desire to understand. ____
20. I alone can decide what people and things and events mean to me. ____
21. I have used my imagination today to enrich my life. ____

For the following items, score:

2 points if I didn't *need* to do it to keep from abusing myself or others.
1 point for YES.
0 points for NO.

CURTAILING SELF-ABUSE AND ABUSE OF OTHERS

If I had the urge to hurt myself or others, or realized that I was hurting myself or others, did I do the following?

24. saw the flashing letters: *HEALING*. ____
25. looked within myself for emotional regulation. ____
26. identified my deepest feelings. ____
27. felt my deepest feelings for 20 seconds. ____
28. changed the meaning. ____
29. felt compassion for myself. ____
30. felt compassion for others. ____
31. Saw a bright red screen in my imagination that read: PLEASE BE KIND. ____

Add up your total score. Then look at the low-scored items and decide which you can improve immediately.

SELF-ESTEEM TRANSFUSION SCHEDULE

Homework Answer Sheet

1.	1.	1.	1.	1.
2.	2.	2.	2.	2.
3.	3.	3.	3.	3.
4.	4.	4.	4.	4.
5.	5.	5.	5.	5.
6.	6.	6.	6.	6.
7.	7.	7.	7.	7.
8.	8.	8.	8.	8.
9.	9.	9.	9.	9.
10.	10.	10.	10.	10.
11.	11.	11.	11.	11.
12.	12.	12.	12.	12.
13.	13.	13.	13.	13.
14.	14.	14.	14.	14.
15.	15.	15.	15.	15.
16.	16.	16.	16.	16.

17.	17.	17.	17.	17.
18.	18.	18.	18.	18.
19.	19.	19.	19.	19.
20.	20.	20.	20.	20.
21.	21.	21.	21.	21.
22.	22.	22.	22.	22.
23.	23.	23.	23.	23.
24.	24.	24.	24.	24.
25.	25.	25.	25.	25.
26.	26.	26.	26.	26.
27.	27.	27.	27.	27.
28.	28.	28.	28.	28.
29.	29.	29.	29.	29.
30.	30.	30.	30.	30.
31.	31.	31.	31.	31.
Total Score	Total Score	Total Score	Total Score	Total Score

1.	1.	1.	1.	1.
2.	2.	2.	2.	2.
3.	3.	3.	3.	3.
4.	4.	4.	4.	4.
5.	5.	5.	5.	5.
6.	6.	6.	6.	6.
7.	7.	7.	7.	7.
8.	8.	8.	8.	8.
9.	9.	9.	9.	9.
10.	10.	10.	10.	10.
11.	11.	11.	11.	11.
12.	12.	12.	12.	12.
13.	13.	13.	13.	13.
14.	14.	14.	14.	14.
15.	15.	15.	15.	15.
16.	16.	16.	16.	16.
17.	17.	17.	17.	17.
18.	18.	18.	18.	18.
19.	19.	19.	19.	19.
20.	20.	20.	20.	20.

21.	21.	21.	21.	21.
22.	22.	22.	22.	22.
23.	23.	23.	23.	23.
24.	24.	24.	24.	24.
25.	25.	25.	25.	25.
26.	26.	26.	26.	26.
27.	27.	27.	27.	27.
28.	28.	28.	28.	28.
29.	29.	29.	29.	29.
30.	30.	30.	30.	30.
31.	31.	31.	31.	31.
Total Score	Total Score	Total Score	Total Score	Total Score

Worksheet 9.7

Building Immunity to the Core Hurts

The purpose of this exercise is to build immunity to the core hurts that all human beings experience. As these hurts are put into words, written down, and said aloud, the more powerful part of the brain dominates, at last healing the wounds from which the feelings emanate. After you write them slowly, say them aloud, slowly and deliberately. The goal is to forge new associations, to help the brain develop healthier ways of processing hurt.

Slowly write out each core hurt *with* its corresponding correction in the second column.

	(Note: *As you write out the correctional statements, feel yourself regulating the feelings. Feel yourself gaining complete control of them.*)
I feel disregarded.	I regard my own feelings.
I feel unimportant.	I am as important as any human being.
I feel accused/guilty.	If I am guilty I will make up for what I've done. If I'm not guilty, I'll forgive my accusers.
I feel powerless.	I have power over my internal experience.
I feel devalued.	I value myself.
I feel rejected.	I accept myself; and I do not see other people's rejection as a reflection of myself.
I feel unlovable.	I am compassionate, which makes me worthy of love.

Worksheet 9.8

Homework Assignment # 11 INNER POWER: Thought and Feeling Conversion

Write a note about a time when you thought that someone made you feel:	Slowly write-out the conversion:
disregarded	"I regard myself." feel: self-regard
unimportant	"I know I'm important." feel: acceptance of my own importance
accused	"I'm worthy of trust, even if she can't give it." feel: compassion for self & accuser
devalued	"No one can *make* me think less of myself." feel: acceptance of personal value
rejected	"I accept myself." feel: disappointment, self-compassion, self-acceptance
powerless	"I don't *need* to exert power outside myself to feel powerful." feel: acceptance of inner-power
unlovable	"If someone doesn't love me, it doesn't mean that I'm not lovable." feel: compassion for self and others

Worksheet 9.9

Homework Assignment # 12
Power over Core Hurts

To protect yourself from the core hurts, it's necessary to build strength in their opposites, to make yourself feel:

important
above accusation
valuable
unrejectable
powerful
lovable

Slowly write out the following:

I'm *lovable* because I'm compassionate.
Doing compassionate things makes me feel lovable.

I'm *powerful* because I'm compassionate.
Doing compassionate things makes me feel powerful.

I'm acceptable because I'm compassionate. (If someone seems to reject me, it's due to what's in his or her head and heart, not mine.)

I'm *valuable* because I'm compassionate.
Doing compassionate things makes me feel valuable.

I'm unoffended by accusation because I'm compassionate.
Doing compassionate things makes me feel above accusation.

I'm *important* because I'm compassionate.

Doing compassionate things makes me feel important.

(The point of this exercise is: The more compassion you feel, the more protected you are from the core hurts. Say each item aloud—it's healing just to hear your voice saying the words.)

Worksheet 9.10

Homework Assignment # 13 Drilling Your New Emotional Regulation Skill

Goals:

1. building self-esteem
2. increasing self-knowledge
3. increasing tolerance of—and immunity to—the core hurts
4. making yourself feel important, above accusation, valuable, unrejectable, lovable

Briefly describe the worst dispute you ever had with your spouse/significant other, parent or child, when you got the angriest, felt the most disregarded, unimportant, devalued, unlovable.

How could this dispute have been better using your new emotional regulation skill?

Worksheet 9.11

Compassionate Morality and Self-Esteem

By now the link between compassionate morality and self-esteem should be clear. An explanation of the psychobiological function of the Attachment Bond will make it clearer.

THE ATTACHMENT BOND: BUILDS THE INNER SELF OF CHILDREN ENHANCES THE INNER SELF OF ADULTS

Attachment is an emotional bond between people in intimate relationships, developing over time from shared emotional experience. It's the *psychobiological glue* that holds us together as families.

Babies need it to survive (or else they fall into anaclitic depression and eventually die). Children need it to thrive.

Attachment connects us to other people, who then provide us with a *mirror of our inner selves.* We learn what we are inside (how important, valuable, acceptable, and lovable we are) by interacting with people we love. Our well-being and our self-esteem are deeply connected to the well-being and self-esteem of those we love.

As the most important attachment emotion, compassion is a crucial element of genuine self-esteem and genuine pride. It is also crucial to the individual development of attachment figures.

Because self-compassion is necessary to sustain compassion for others, all immorality and all deficits in genuine pride and self-esteem begin with a *failure of self-compassion.*

When we enhance those attached to us, we enhance the self.

When we devalue or abuse those attached to us, we devalue and abuse the self.

When we devalue and abuse the self, we devalue and abuse those attached to us.

Compassion (for self and others), morality, and self-esteem are each dependent on the other. We can't sustain one without the others.

As it becomes a central part of your identity that you are a compassionate, moral person, your self-esteem soars. Each act of morality is yet another injection of self-esteem and genuine pride.

Worksheet 9.12

Homework Assignment # 14
Building Your Compassion Shield

In medieval times, knights engraved on their shields and protective armor symbols of the things that they believed protected them, made them strong, and helped them to do their best.

You can build such a shield with compassion. Your *Compassion Shield* will protect you from any abusive behavior by others and empower you to be as strong as possible to avoid any accidental (and, of course, purposeful) abuse of others.

For your Shield of Compassion, make a list of your strengths, assets, accomplishments, and your best qualities—the things that make you strong.

1.
2.
3.
4.
5.
6.
7.
8.
9.
10.

Review your list, applying heavy doses of *self-compassion* and *compassion for others*. Now recreate the list below and see if it has become stronger.

1.
2.
3.
4.
5.
6.
7.
8.
9.
10.

Worksheet 9.13

Power Within, Empowerment Without

Now that you have learned self-regulation skills, it seems more obvious that genuine *power* is *internal*, equivalent to a *solid, well-integrated sense of self.* Now you can avoid the confusion that many people suffer in the mistaken belief that power can be achieved by making other people do things. This mistake leads inevitably to feelings of *powerlessness*, a constant source of guilt, shame, anxiety, and anger. Attempting to exert power over others only *weakens* internal power.

However, one special kind of interpersonal power enhances internal power: *empowerment* of loved ones. *Empowerment* means giving someone the right and the confidence to find a solution that is beneficial to all involved parties.

RESOLVING DISPUTES

Goal: Each person feels good about himself/herself; each feels important, regarded, respected, valuable.

It's okay to disagree, to see things differently, to feel differently about something; unless it's about abuse, rarely is one person completely right and the other completely wrong.

***Empowering loved ones is a* source of personal power.**

"Here's the problem: What do you think is the best solution?"

If you disagree with the solution, don't attack or put down the other person.

1. Validate the suggestion as a *possible* solution.
2. State your reasons for disagreeing.
3. Solicit another soultion.

This approach unites the family in *solution-finding* (rather than struggling for power and advantage). It opens the door for creative solutions and enriches the experience for everyone.

Make a sincere attempt to understand your partner's personal goals and preferences.

Example: Family members rarely share the same tolerance for mess (or compulsion for neatness). This often results in a no-win power struggle with everybody feeling put upon and resentful. A sincere attempt to understand both points of view is necessary:

> "I know it's a problem to carry your glass into the kitchen, cause you like to feel like you can relax in your own home. (And I appreciate it when you do carry in your glass.) I'm not trying to put a power trip on you, but it's important to me that the house look neat. What do you think is a fair solution?"
>
> "I don't really mind carrying in my glass, you just hassle me about it if I forget. I don't *try* to forget."
>
> "If you make a sincere effort to remember to carry in your glass, I'll make a sincere effort not to hassle you if you really do forget. Is that fair?"

Allow each person to set his or her personal goals and preferences when they do not impinge on the rights of others.

Examples: A spouse's personal goal is to improve the relationship with his or her family. This must be honored as his or her personal goal.

A spouse prefers not to go shopping. This should be honored as a personal preference, so long as the burden of shopping is shared equally most of the time.

Worksheet 9.14

Building Power Within

To build a sense of power within, we need to develop strategies to make ourselves feel important, valuable, above accusation, unrejectable, powerful, and loveable.

Please circle as many strategies as apply to you.

1. To make myself feel valuable, I

a. hurt my loved ones b. become angry c. think that I'm better than or superior to him or her d. try to control her or him e. value my loved ones and myself.

2. To make myself feel above accusation, I

a. hurt my loved ones b. become angry c. accuse back d. think that I'm better than or superior to him or her e. understand why he or she is accusing me f. try to find a solution to the problem causing the accusation.

3. To make myself feel unrejectable, I

a. hurt my loved ones b. become angry c. reject them before they can reject me d. force them not to reject me e. think that I'm better than or superior to him or her f. refuse to reject myself.

4. To make myself feel powerful, I

a. hurt my loved ones b. become angry c. try to control them d. think that I'm better than or superior to him or her e. try to feel powerless f. empower myself and my loved ones.

5. To make myself feel loveable, I

a. hurt my loved ones b. become angry c. think that I'm better than or superior to him or her d. consider their perspective e. feel compassion for myself and for my loved ones f. allow myself to love g. show my love.

Worksheet 9.15

The Heart Disease of Families, The # 1 Family-Killer: Power Struggles

When one person wins, everybody loses.

You cannot diminish or hurt people you love without diminishing and hurting yourself.

You cannot diminish or hurt your spouse without diminishing and hurting your children.

You cannot enhance and empower your spouse or children without enhancing and empowering yourself.

Worksheet 9.16

Power Struggles

Please circle the correct answer.

1. Which gives you more power?

Winning a dispute
or
Resolving a dispute in such a way that all parties feel the best they can feel?

2. You cannot win, if someone you love loses.

True or False

3. Which gives you more power?

Dominating your spouse or children
or
Empowering your spouse or children

4. Do you empower your loved ones by:

Telling them what to do (or not to do)
By helping them come up with a solution?

5. What is genuine personal power?

Power over your internal experience
or
The ability to bully, intimidate, or use force against a spouse or child?

6. What motivates a person to control someone else?

Fear of a mistake? Fear of chaos? Fear of feeling something he or she doesn't want to feel? The irrational belief that there's only one right way to do things.

Worksheet 9.17

Power in Attachment Relationships

Internalize Control of the Reward, so that the primary reward lies within you and not in your attachment figures.

Power lies in compassion, regardless of whether it's returned.
Power lies in loving, not in how it's returned.
Power lies in self-disclosure and self-discovery, not in your spouse's reaction.

You empower yourself by refusing to reject yourself, even if your spouse seems to reject you.

Worksheet 9.18

The Secret of Avoiding Power Struggles

A mode of self is a way or style of thinking, feeling, and behaving. Every adult human being has *Weak Modes* of self as well as *Power Modes* of self.

WEAK MODES of Self	POWER MODES of Self
Helpless	Competent
Dependent	Growth/creative
Depressive	Healing/nurturing
Destructive	Compassionate

In trying to settle disputes with parents, spouses, and children, which modes of self do you want to activate in yourself?

Which do you want to activate in your attachment figure?

The surest way to avoid power struggles and make home life peaceful, loving, and functional, is to evoke the Power Modes of everyone in the family. This can only be done in the Power Modes of self.

10 The Compassion Workshop, Module Five: Negotiating Attachment Relationships; Module Six: Moving Toward the Future

MODULE FIVE: NEGOTIATING ATTACHMENT RELATIONSHIPS

The first thing that clients are asked to do in this section of treatment is prepare a homework assignment that evaluates the current status of their attachment bonds (Worksheet 10.1). This should not be attempted earlier in treatment for a simple reason. Before emotional regulation techniques are learned and some skill in interpersonal empowerment is developed, relationship evaluation will be negatively motivated to reduce guilt, shame, and fear of abandonment. At this point in treatment, clients can more realistically evaluate the potential of their attachment relationships to enrich their lives.

VALUE, RESPECT, TRUST, AND LOVE

Worksheet 10.2, Time Dimensions for Recovery, sets parameters for recovering from hurt within attachment relationships. This should be presented to clients as a method of labeling behaviors and emotions to help them recognize behavioral tendencies with high risk of relapse.

Damaged attachment relationships falter in recovery when the parties try to force themselves to renew complete trust prematurely. Due to the priority processing given to painful memories, the brain will not allow total trust to return quickly to relationships that have known hurt, no matter how much the parties might desire it. However, the hyper-vigilance of clients in recovery can be alleviated if they have an idea of when to expect that trust is most likely to falter. When we get burned on the stove, we don't walk around all day worrying about getting burned again. Rather, the nervous flinch comes when we're near enough to feel the heat. In attachment relationships, the psychological flinch comes when intimacy is renewed, perhaps in a gentle or passionate embrace, a kiss, a brief touch. At this inopportune moment the brain's alarm goes off, quite unexpectedly and regrettably: "The last time I let down my defenses like this, I got hurt!"

Attempts at intimacy-renewal hold the greatest risk of rejection for previously abusive attachment figures. Therapists need to help both ex-abusers and victims to understand that a certain amount of holding back is a normal response, a part of the healing process, and a quirk of the way the brain processes hurtful information. They must know that this involuntary reaction will pass, but only when preceded by a period of value and support. In the meantime, the former abuser and victim need help to perceive the involuntary flinch as other than rejection, which could push back the healing process to square one. Trust and love are future orientations toward which attachment figures must strive through the firm establishment of value and respect.

The double-edged sabre at the heart of attachment relationships—Fear of Abandonment and Fear of Engulfment—is introduced in Worksheet 10.3.

Dysfunctional ways of coping with the two-horned beast of abandonment and engulfment anxiety ring all too familiarly to family therapists. The first of these is smothering the fear of abandonment with a continual push for more closeness, creating a role known in relationship dynamics as the "pursuer." The common strategy to regulate the fear of engulfment—keeping others at a distance—is a role known in relationship dynamics as the "distancer." Thus one partner continually wants more closeness than the other can tolerate. This interaction dynamic (described in Worksheet 10.4), though usually discussed in the clinical literature of couples counseling, presents all too often in parent–child and in adult child–elder parent interactions as well.

Neither pursuer nor distancer self-regulates abandonment or engulfment anxiety. Rather, each relies on the other to set personal boundaries and limits. All pursuers occasionally want some privacy. Yet they pursue even then, partly out of habit and partly out of fear that reduction in pursuit might indicate a loss of fervor and send the "wrong message" to the distancer. It might even portend loss of identity as the pursuer, that is, the one responsible for intimacy and emotional vitality in the relationship. Similarly, the distancer occasionally wants more intimacy, but fears that it might seem uncharacteristic, or that it will only bring on even more vigorous and troublesome pursuit by the insatiable pursuer.

Fear of engulfment has the effect of making every intimate relationship seem abusive, as intimacy itself seems dangerous. The inability to discern abusive from nonabusive intimate behavior actually increases the risk for those with exaggerated engulfment-anxiety to fall into abusive relationships. This tragic condition owes itself to the palpable defenses erected by engulfment-anxious persons. Nonabusive people, that is, *most* people, respect those defenses and keep a comfortable distance, whereas abusive persons smash through them, to "rescue" engulfment-anxious persons from themselves. Those afflicted with engulfment anxiety do less to *attract* abusers than to keep everyone else at emotional distance. This is why the customary treatment of people who repeatedly enter abusive relationships—establishing firmer "boundaries"—often fails. The help that former victims need in this area centers on the gradual and incremental *letting down* of barriers, enough to discover the nonabusive majority. Experience with the normal will make the abusive stand out like sore thumbs and thus lower the risk of entering into abusive relationships. Fear of abandonment has a similar but different effect of blurring boundaries, making the abuser's indifference to personal boundaries seem indistinguishable from compassionate caring.

Worksheet 10.4 shows clients how to regulate fear of engulfment and fear of abandonment.

Regulating the amount of closeness and distance in attachment relationships runs a high risk of continuing the Pendulum of Pain (Chapter 3). The individual's varying need for closeness (let alone the varying needs of each attachment figure), in tandem with making requests for distance seem like rejection (or taking them that way), thrusts couples into a rigid and painful rejection-withdrawal interactive pattern. Thus the common response in an abusive relationship, when one person attempts to embrace the other: "You didn't want to hug me yesterday when I wanted to, so get away now!"

Depending on the ability of each party to tolerate actual or seeming rejection, this pattern of interaction becomes a breeding ground for abuse.

Worksheet 10.5, with a companion homework assignment, gives clients ways of regulating closeness and distance.

CONFLICT RESOLUTION

At this point in the treatment, clients have evaluated the strength and resilience of their attachment bond and have begun to develop skills to:

1. regulate abandonment and engulfment anxiety;
2. regulate closeness-distance comfort levels;
3. leave the Pendulum of Pain.

Now they are ready to learn ways to negotiate differences with one another, while protecting and enhancing the attachment bond. This involves forming an alliance among all attachment participants to heal the hurt beneath the anger and to make solution-seeking a joint venture (Worksheet 10.6). In other words, though they may disagree in content (and, almost invariably, about the causes of problems), they seek solutions in allegiance.

Worksheet 10.7 offers clients a formula for handling disputes with loved ones. Worksheet 10.8 establishes rules for conflict resolution.

The most formidable barrier to "re-alliance" and establishment of a deeper intimacy is resentment. A series of handouts, collected in Worksheet 10.9, explains the dynamics of resentment and gives practical advice on overcoming it.

Worksheet 10.10 helps clients decide how much intimacy they want and how much they can reasonably expect to get in their present relationships. I ask clients to apply the Intimacy Test to all their present, past, and future relationships.

Nearing the end of treatment, clients should be asked to consolidate gains (Worksheet 10.11). In my experience with attachment abusers and victims, they internalize and retain material much better when they can sum it up, both in writing and orally in the treatment session. Actually, this constitutes a major ego trip for the therapist, as you see that clients have in fact internalized and retained much more than you may have thought or even hoped.

MODULE SIX: MOVING TOWARD THE FUTURE

Module Six begins with the development of strategies for relapse-prevention (Worksheet 10.12). This includes a series of criteria to serve as measures of gradual decline in well-being, with specific suggestions to reverse any downward trend before it leads to relapse.

By this point in treatment, 90% of the clients in the Compassion Workshop have gained control of abusive tendencies. Now they must be reminded that the experience of abuse, especially violence, whether as victim or perpetrator, creates a lasting disposition for further abusive behavior. There is some evidence that messages of pain are transmitted and processed in separate neural networks due to its importance to survival (Ornstein & Sobel, 1990). This priority processing may be sufficient to give reflexive responses to pain—anger and violence—priority status as well. The metaphor of the *bite of the vampire* informs clients that once they have experienced abuse and violence, they bear the fangs of the vampire and will have to manage the urge to inflict harm on those closest to them. Having the fangs of the vampire presents a problem only if clients forget that they have them, that is, stop doing the self-regulation exercises that keep them in control of their internal experience. If they resist the urge to fool themselves, if they remain aware of their potential for abuse, they can keep the fangs retracted without fear of hurting those they kiss.

HEALING LETTERS OF APOLOGY

Letters of apology (Worksheet 10.13), the final assignment of the Compassion Workshop, provides clients with a way of making a clear demarcation between their self-destructive styles of thinking, feeling, and behaving of the past, and the self-building styles they've learned in the present. Completion of the assignment promises to close the door on the past and open the door to the future. It forges a new identity for willing clients as complex, growth-oriented, compassionate, healing persons. The letter should serve as a kind of blueprint for reversing periods of relapse. The content must recount the steps of the client's recovery, including what needs to be done to advance recovery. One objective of the assignment is to create a document that can be read during vulnerable periods in the future, to tell clients what to do for renewed progress and inspire them to fulfill their emerging identity as compassionate persons.

Clients tend to hate this exercise when first assigned. But the vast majority find it a wonderfully healing process in the doing.

On the final day of treatment, clients read their letters aloud. If the treatment modality is conjoint or group, other members are asked to give feedback on how well the letter meets the requirements and objectives of the assignment.

RELAPSE-PREVENTION PACKET

Clients should be given a relapse-prevention packet that recapitulates key strategies used throughout the Compassion Workshop, covering the points mentioned in Worksheet 10.14. Detailed information, including phone numbers of contacts and social supports, as well as all completed homework assignments, should be provided in a convenient folder for each client.

Worksheet 10.1

Homework Assignment # 15
The Attachment Bond

The following are questions you must answer from deep in your heart.

How much do you love this person?

Is the attachment bond between you a strong one?

Or is it maintained by habit, convenience, or coercion?

Is the damage done to the relationship repairable?

Do you *want* to repair it?

How can it be repaired?

How will you know that it is being repaired? (There must be positive improvement, not just, "We don't fight as much," or, "He (or she) isn't so mean to me anymore."

What will you do differently when it is repaired? (You can start doing it now to control your own recovery.)

How can you go forward, growing from the hurt of the past? (You must grow to heal, whether your loved ones grow with you or not.)

Worksheet 10.2

Time Dimensions for Recovery

THE PAST	THE PRESENT	THE FUTURE
danger	*safety*	*safety*
blame	*responsibility*	*responsibility*
insulting	respect	trust
injured feelings	value	love
emotional battering	support	support
physical harm	mutual growth	mutual growth
police, court, jail		

Know which reactions are from the past and *label* them as leftovers of the past. Try to live in the present and look toward the future. *If a thought, feeling, or behavior is a "leftover" of the past, acknowledge, validate, and change it.*

Blaming belongs in the past. *Blaming* and threats to *safety* will bring back the past. They must be replaced with responsibility, respect, value, support, and mutual growth.

Due to the special way the brain regards the possible recurrence of pain (e.g., flinching near a stove once you've been burned), it is unrealistic to expect *trust* and *love* to return immediately in relationships that have been abusive. No matter how much you might want to trust someone who has hurt you, your brain will resist fully letting down defenses. *This is an involuntary reaction.* Trust and love returns quite gradually, and only when followed by a period of *value* and *respect.*

Trust is not an all or nothing thing. You can have 10% trust that develops into 20% trust, 50% trust, 75%, and so on, until it gradually reaches 100%.

In the meantime, all parties must understand that the seeming rejection implied by diminished trust and intimacy is actually rejection of the *past,* abusive relationship, and not of the *present,* evolving relationship. This knowledge will prevent setback and shorten the time required for replenishment of trust, love, and uninhibited intimacy.

Worksheet 10.3

The Great Threat of Intimacy

Two great fears reside deep in the core self of most human beings.

Fear of Engulfment: If she (or he) gets too close, the self will be:

exposed and vulnerable
overwhelmed
disintegrated or
absorbed by another self.

Fear of Abandonment: If she or he moves too far away, the self will:

lose identity
lose value
disintegrate.

Although every human being has these two great fears, they are intensified by childhood and adult attachment experience. For example, *rejected or neglected* children are likely to have an exaggerated fear of abandonment, while *abused or dominated* children or those *not loved for who they really are,* have exaggerated fear of engulfment—if loved ones get too close they will hurt and overwhelm the self.

How to tell fear of abandonment from genuinely missing someone: If you feel anxious and terribly lonely when not with that person, but when you are with him or her, it really isn't all that great, fear of abandonment powers your relationship.

How to tell fear of engulfment from the mere desire for a little privacy and distance: If you can't wait to get away from that person, but when you're away from him or her, you start missing him or her, fear of engulfment powers your relationship.

THE DESPERATE DANCE OF PURSUER-DISTANCER

There are two common ways of coping with fear of abandonment and fear of engulfment:

- smothering it with closeness—the *pursuer*
- keeping others at a distance—the *distancer*

One member will continually want more closeness and intimacy than the other can tolerate. The *pursuer* sets up all sorts of manipulations for closeness and intimacy, whereas the *distancer* confounds and distracts from these, using other people, work, alcohol or drugs, TV, hobbies, etc., as distancing strategies.

Neither the pursuer or distancer self-regulates fear of abandonment and fear of engulfment; each relies on the other to set limits. So pursuers never have to worry about how much closeness they really want; they rely on distancers to decide how much they will get. Distancers never have to decide on how much closeness they want, rather, they occasionally relent in their rejection "for the sake of the pursuer."

Two great problems:

1. The pursuer-distancer dance always ends in *rejection.*
2. The accumulated shame—of rejecting a loved one and of being rejected by a loved one—takes on a life of its own, stimulating anger and causing great damage to the attachment bond.

Typically, pursuers stop pursuing when the weight of continual rejection becomes too great. When they back away, they often stimulate distancers to begin their own pursuit in a dramatic role-reversal. (Distancers typically fall in love with their mates as they are leaving.)

Though most typical of relationships between lovers, the pursuer-distancer dance can afflict *any* attachment relationship. A common example is the adult child rigorously pursuing the love, acceptance, or approval of a rejecting or aloof or preoccupied parent. This tends to be a same-sex phenomenon (though certainly not always), with adult sons pursuing distant fathers and adult daughters pursuing withholding or critical mothers.

The pursuit by parents of adult children is often powered by guilt over childhood neglect or abuse. The parent whose parental years were dominated by alcoholism, work, other children, depression, affairs, etc., is especially susceptible to this sort of pursuit.

Needy parents often find their young children and adolescents distancing in an effort to maintain sufficient space for the development of their own personalities, values, opinions, and interests.

Young children and adolescents pursue absent and distancing parents to the best of their limited abilities, working hard through school performance, cuteness, athletics, or any other means to earn their parents' love.

Worksheet 10.4

Regulating Fear of Abandonment and Fear of Engulfment

The only way out of the painful and frustrating dance of the pursuer-distancer is for each person to self-regulate fear of abandonment and fear of engulfment.

Fear of abandonment and fear of engulfment become worse problems when we expect or desire our loved ones to regulate them for us. When not self-regulated, fear of abandonment keeps us in bad relationships (and prevents them from becoming better), while fear of engulfment keeps us out of good relationships.

At heart, both the *fear of engulfment* and the *fear of abandonment* are fears of losing control of internal experience. Therefore, a greater sense of control, through self-regulation of feelings and self-esteem, alleviates the fear of losing control.

Fear of abandonment is fear of feeling incomplete without the other.

Regulation:

1. Do *H*EALS, (If this person fails to love me, it does not mean that I'm unimportant, not valuable, rejectable, unlovable.)
2. Realize that you can be disappointed, sad, and lonely, but the self is not at stake, there is no loss of self-esteem, if this person fails to love you.

Fear of engulfment is fear of feeling overwhelmed by the other.

This is harder to regulate due to veiled feelings of rejection and abandonment. (If people get too close they will see the real me that is unlovable and that cannot love.)

Regulation:

1. Steps 1 and 2 above, to regulate hidden fear of abandonment.
2. *Acceptance that:*
   a. Everyone has a part of the self that is not lovable and that cannot love.
   b. The lovable and loving parts of the self are more important to relationships.
   c. You can regulate any internal experience.
   d. The self is too solid and well-integrated to be overwhelmed or absorbed by another.

Worksheet 10.5

Closeness Regulation

After the initial, romantic phase of the relationship, men and women seldom agree on how close they want to be and how far apart they want to be.

The usual result is the Pursuer-Distancer dance, wherein one partner tries to be closer, and the other withdraws to maintain a steady distance between them. This process can be filled with frustration, sorrow, and resentment on the part of both partners.

In everyone, the degree of desired closeness:

1. varies greatly from week to week, day to day, even moment to moment;
2. may be cyclical;
3. depends on stressors (though some people want more closeness under stress while others want more distance);
4. is governed by two great fears (both intensified by childhood rejection, neglect, or abuse):
   fear of abandonment,
   fear of engulfment.

DYSFUNCTIONAL DISTANCE REGULATION:

1. using anger as a distance regulator
2. interpreting distance regulation as rejection

FUNCTIONAL (GROWTH ORIENTED) CLOSENESS REGULATION:

1. recognizing and respecting one another's varying needs and desires for closeness and distance;
2. it's okay to want closeness, it's okay to want distance;
3. communicating directly about closeness-regulation.

Homework Assignment # 17

Closeness/Distance Regulation

1. How often is anger used as a distance regulator in your house?

2. How else can you regulate closeness and distance?

3. How do you regulate fear of abandonment?

4. How do you regulate fear of engulfment?

Worksheet 10.6

Forming an Alliance to Heal the Hurt Beneath the Anger

Goals:

1. Stop attending to one another's anger, and attend to the hurt beneath the anger.

2. Find ways to support one another in struggles outside the relationship.

3. Concentrate on enhancing the attachment bond between you.

4. Make attacks on the attachment bond *off-limits*.

5. Realize that you're on the same side.

How can you accomplish # 1?

How can you accomplish # 2?

(Think of a dispute that turned into a hurtful argument—how could you have supported your spouse, children, or parents?)

How can you accomplish # 3?

How can you accomplish # 4?

(Avoid threats to abandon or engulf.)

How can you accomplish #5?

Worksheet 10.7

Getting the Understanding You Want

The secret to *getting understanding* lies in giving it. To remove barriers to being understood, in every problematic exchange with an attachment figure, ask yourself:

What do I want from my attachment figure in this interaction?

1. Do I want him/her to regulate my feelings?

If *yes, stop* and do *HEALS*.
If no, go to # 2

2. Do I want him/her to understand what I am thinking, feeling, doing?

If *no, stop* and re-examine your goals.
If *yes*, go to # 3

3. Do I want him/her to listen to me and validate my feelings?

If *yes*, go to # 3-A

3-A. Am I listening to and validating his/her feelings?

If *no, listen and validate,* then go to # 4
If *yes*, go to # 4

4. Do I want this person to do something for me?

If *yes*, go to # 4-A
If *no*, go to # 5

4-A. Will this person doing this for me make me feel more competent, creative, self-nurturing, and compassionate?

If *no*, stop and work *HEALS*.
If *yes*, go to # 5.

5. Have I discussed this in a respectful, nonabusive, nonthreatening, nonblaming, nondefensive, nonmartyr way?

If *no*, call time out and try again in a nonabusive, nonthreatening, nonblaming way.
If *yes*, go to # 6.

6. If the barriers continue because the other feels unable to discuss the issues right now, ask, in a respectful, nonabusive, nonthreatening, nonblaming, nondefensive, nonmartyr way why he/she can't respond at this time. Set a specific time when he/she can respond.

Worksheet 10.8

Inner Power, Interpersonal Power, Conflict Resolution

The Cardinal Rules:

1. Each party must self-regulate anger to allow negotiation on the issue rather than the core hurts that cause anger.

2. The ultimate goal of solution-seeking must be that everyone feels as good about himself and herself as possible, everyone feels important, regarded, valued, respected. Anything less than this only makes the problem worse.

3. a.) Empower yourself through recognition of your competence, growth, creativity, nurturing, and compassion. b.) Empower your loved ones by supporting their competence, growth, creativity, and compassion.

   Although the cardinal rules alone will help you solve most problems, here are few additional rules to help settle disputes. But conflict resolution skills can only correct deficits in communication. You have to *want* to communicate, and you have to *care* about what your loved ones feel for any attempts at conflict resolution to work.

4. *Narrow* the dispute as much as possible, focusing on specific behavior at specific times. Don't bring-in past hurts or offenses. Don't say "you always" or "you never". Be *specific.*

5. Talk only about behavior, never the "personality" of loved ones. Example: "I felt uncomfortable when you

said that," not, "You bitch!" Or, "You're a cold, inconsiderate person!" Example: "I have a different perception," not, "You're a liar," or, "You're crazy," or "You make up things in your head."

6. Make "I" statements. "I feel upset when you say that," rather than, "You make me angry." In the first case you own the feeling and have power over it; in the second, you blame the feeling on your attachment figure, rendering yourself powerless.

7. Create new options to negotiate whenever possible. Example: "I can't get home in time to go to dinner, but we'll have time to see a movie."

8. If new options are not possible, negotiate, *with mutual respect* and *sincerity*, until you can decide to whom the issue is more important. For instance, it's important for her to go out that night and relax after a tense day, and it's important for him to go home and relax after an exhausting day. "I know you've had a tense day, and if I weren't so beat, I'd go out with you to help you unwind. But I'm just too tired." Note: The way to communicate importance is with passion or conviction and with honesty and sincerity. Anger prevents communication of these or any of your deeper feelings; the function of anger is to cover up deeper feelings for the purpose of defense/attack.

Remember, the key to conflict resolution is self-regulation, self-empowerment, and empowerment of your spouse or child or parent, and a *sincere* desire to have everyone feel as good about themselves as possible.

Worksheet 10.9

Resolution or Giving-In

What happens when a spouse gives in and goes along, just to keep the peace, or to avoid a hassle, or because he/she is too tired to argue?

a. everyone feels good about themselves

or

b. the creation of resentment and hidden hostility that can last indefinitely

RESENTMENT

Resentment may be the most complex of all human emotions. The result of every power struggle, it is extremely difficult to resolve, due to its many components. It may account for most of the ill-feeling we experience; it never really ends.

Components of resentment:

1. *regret*
2. *remorse*
3. *shame*
4. *self-anger*
5. *anger* at opponent in power-struggle
6. *anger at others* in general

Example:

I agreed to have my brother-in-law, whom I don't like, move in with us, because my wife wanted it. I keep noticing things about his behavior that irritate me. I take it out on my wife—if it wasn't for her, I wouldn't have to put up with him.

1. I *regret* my brother-in-law moving in.
2. I'm *sorry* that I misled my wife into thinking I could stand it.
3. I feel *shame* that I can't do this for her, so I continually look for justification of my failure—he snores, he has a poor sense of humor, he doesn't comb his hair right, etc.
4. I'm *angry at her* for not appreciating how much of a bother this would be and for not understanding me. I'm angry at her for not wanting what I want, for not feeling the way I do about this, and for not agreeing with me.
5. I'm *angry at myself* for failing to realize how much bother it would be and for not being assertive about my true feelings.
6. Because resentment puts me in a bad mood, I get *angry at other people* about little things, like traffic, the news, my team losing, the baby crying, the phone ringing, etc.

PREVENTING RESENTMENT

Although hard to resolve, resentment is much easier to prevent:

1. Resolve disputes, power-struggles, and decisions, with closure. Be sure you can say:

> I'm convinced that this is the best thing I can do, at this time, and I *commit* myself to making it work.

2. Feel good about the resolution.

This means *expressing shame:*

> I know it sounds childish, but I'm afraid that if your brother moves in, I won't get enough of your time, and I care about having time with you.

NOTE: If you don't express shame, it undermines any attempt to make the solution work, as well as any attempt at true intimacy.

3. Reward yourself with a feeling of well-being for doing the right thing, whatever that turns out to be.

4. Accept responsibility for your decision.

   With responsibility, you regulate your own experience.

   With resentment, your feelings are in the power of someone else.

5. If it turns out that you made a mistake, make the most of it:

   I made a mistake in *my* decision, but what can I do to grow and to learn from the mistake?

OTHER KINDS OF RESENTMENT, CAUSED BY

1. not getting to make a decision:

   We're told, "You do this."

2. the opinions and expectations of others

3. not getting expected or desired:

   a. help
   b. appreciation
   c. consideration
   d. reward.

STEPS IN RESOLVING THESE KINDS OF RESENTMENT

1. Say explicitly what you desire/expect.
2. Internalize (control) your own appreciation, consideration, and reward.

What could prevent you from doing these things?

THE CHAIN OF RESENTMENT

The continuous nature of resentment creates a chain-like, self-linking bond. Past resentments seem to attract present offenses, forming an ever-longer and heavier chain.

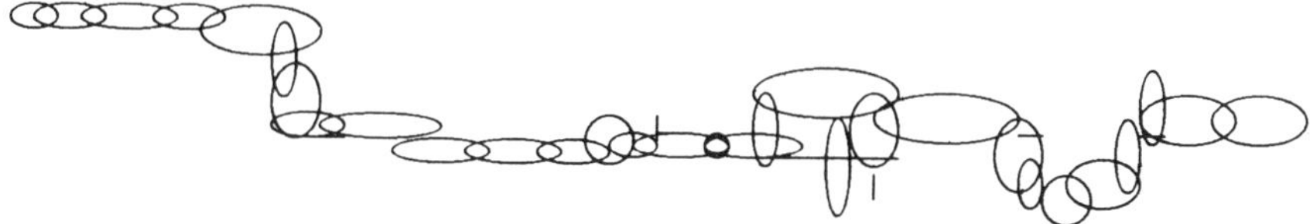

The Chain of Resentment makes it almost impossible to resolve individual points, because each link on the chain connects it to all the others, so that failing to wash the dishes has the emotional import of each and every other link.

To make matters worse, The Chain of Resentment does not distinguish important matters from petty or trivial ones when the petty or trivial matters stimulate core hurts. If it makes you feel unlovable, "I forgive (or resent) you for not doing the dishes," can share significance with, "I forgive (or resent) you for pressuring me to leave my child." The tremendous effort required to drag the Chain of Resentment through life makes us hyper-vigilant for possible offenses, lest they "sneak up" on us. This creates frequent sour moods and an atmosphere wherein no offense is too trivial or too unrealistic to be added as yet another link to the chain of resentment. In other words, like bacteria in a laboratory culture, *resentment breeds resentment.* So we will find reasons for resentment in the daily newspaper, in traffic patterns, in a dearth of parking places, in the temperature of the drinking water, in other people's tastes, thoughts, opinions, feelings, and so on.

BEARING THE CHAIN

To appreciate how resentment affects you, make a list of all the things about your attachment relationships that make you resentful. (If you are honest and thorough, your list will contain many petty and trivial matters, as well as nontrivial ones.) From a hardware store, buy the kind of chain that allows you to add or subtract links with a simple snapping motion. (If you can't find such a chain, buy a bunch of heavy nails.) For each item on your resentment list, add a link to the chain (or drop in five nails). Put the chain (or nails) in a sturdy bag. *Carry the bag around with you constantly.* This means taking it everywhere, to work, to the store, to the bathroom, to get the mail—*everywhere!* This is precisely what we do with resentment.

When you can stand the weight of the bag no longer, get rid of a link (or bunch of nails) for each item on your resentment list that you let go.

BREAKING THE CHAIN

The first thing to realize about the terrible Chain of Resentment is that we don't *have to* feel it. The experience of resentment is a *choice* we make.

The second thing to realize is that the Chain of Resentment binds the *self* more than anyone else. Breaking the chain of resentment means unburdening the *self*, setting the *self* free.

There are three ways of letting go of resentment, two passive and one active. The first way is just like getting rid of one of the links in the sack of chains—we realize how terrible it is to carry through life and simply decide to get rid of it. The second passive way is through compassion. The *active* way is through the very opposite of resentment: *forgiveness.*

COMPASSION AND FORGIVENESS

The relationship between compassion and forgiveness is subtle and complex. Often times, forgiveness is the behavioral enactment of compassion. Forgiveness is an interaction, a behavioral exchange between two or more persons, whereas compassion can be experienced alone, in private and from afar. However, we cannot have genuine forgiveness without genuine compassion.

Just as we cannot sustain compassion for others without self-compassion, we cannot forgive others without *self-forgiveness.* The power of forgiveness, like all genuine power, originates *within.*

Forgiveness *does not mean condoning or overlooking* the offense. Forgiveness means letting go of the *compulsion to punish* or *reject,* in the realization that we cannot harm others, particularly those we love, without harming the self.

FORGIVING THE SELF

The toxic shame component of resentment stimulates the core hurts. Forgiveness of self means forgiving the vulnerability of the self. Wounds within the self must be bathed in self-compassion to prepare for the healing of self-forgiveness.

Remember, the Chain of Resentment does not distinguish important matters from petty or trivial ones when the petty or trivial matters stimulate core hurts. If it makes you feel unlovable, "I forgive (or resent) you for not doing the dishes," can share significance with, "I forgive (or resent) you for pressuring me to leave my child."

Write out each of the following, slowly. And then, slowly, say them aloud.

- I forgive myself for feeling unimportant.
- I forgive myself for feeling disregarded.
- I forgive myself for feeling accused, guilty, untrustworthy.
- I forgive myself for feeling devalued.

- I forgive myself for feeling rejected, unacceptable.
- I forgive myself for feeling unlovable.

FORGIVING OTHERS

- I forgive you for reminding me that I sometimes feel unimportant.
- I forgive you for reminding me that I sometimes feel disregarded.
- I forgive you for reminding me that I sometimes feel accused, guilty, untrustworthy.
- I forgive you for reminding me that I sometimes feel devalued.
- I forgive you for reminding me that I sometimes feel rejected, unacceptable.
- I forgive you for reminding me that I sometimes feel unlovable.

LOOKING FOR EXCUSES TO FORGIVE

Preoccupation with the Chain of Resentment can be replaced by preoccupation with forgiveness. Then we will look for excuses to forgive, to experience the internal well-being of forgiveness. Then we happily discover that forgiveness is a profound expression of the powerful *Healing/Nurturing* mode of self.

RESENTMENT LIST

You must be absolutely honest and put down everything you resent about your attachment figures. Make a separate list for each attachment figure.

I resent:

1.
2.

3.
4.
5.
7.
8.
9.
10.
11.
12.
13.
14.
15.
16.
17.
18.
19.

FORGIVENESS LIST

List each of the items on your resentment list for which you can forgive yourself (for feeling unimportant, disregarded, accused, guilty, untrustworthy, devalued, rejected, unlovable). Then, and only then, can you forgive your attachment figure. (Example: I forgive myself for feeling devalued when my spouse forgot my birthday. My personal value does not depend on the forgetfulness of others. I forgive my spouse for forgetting my birthday.)

I forgive:

1.
2.
3.
4.
5.
6.
7.
8.

9.
10.
11.
12.
13.
14.
15.
16.
17.
18.
19.

Worksheet 10.10

The Requirements of Intimacy

The emotional-regulation techniques you're learning make it possible to have closer and more intimate relationships. You can have as much or as little intimacy in your relationship as you decide. The important thing is that both partners agree and get their needs met.

Intimacy requires:

1. *Caring* about who a person is, caring about what he or she *thinks and feels*, not what you think he or she should think and feel.

This means caring when he or she feels bad about something. It means respecting your differences.

2. *Self-Disclosure:* This means not hiding, or feeling *afraid* to disclose, what you really think and what you really feel. It means freely revealing anything about which you feel ashamed. Such emotional exposure is healing and draws you closer together as you work through any conflicts.

Intimacy Test:

a. Do you want to accept that your partner has thoughts, beliefs, preferences, and feelings that differ from yours? Can you respect those differences? Can you cherish them? Can you accept them without trying to change them?
b. Can you disclose *anything* about yourself, including your deepest thoughts and feelings, without fear of rejection or misunderstanding?
c. Is the message of your relationship, "grow, expand, create, disclose, reveal?" Or is it, "hide, conceal, think only in certain ways, behave only in certain ways, feel only certain things?"

d. Does this relationship offer both parties optimal growth? Can you both develop into the greatest persons you can be?

3. *Protecting the Attachment Bond*

This means trying, especially in disputes, not to threaten *abandonment* or *engulfment:*

Disputes must be about *behavior,* not about the *person.*

Example:

"I have a problem with this behavior. What can we do about it?"

Not:

"You're stupid."
"You're hopeless, you always mess up!"
"You're a bad boy!"
"You son of a bitch!"

How anger attacks the attachment bond:

The biological function of anger is to hurt, ward off, drive away, or intimidate.

This natural function of anger, when turned on intimates, stimulates fear of abandonment, fear of engulfment, shame, and anger.

How compassion protects the attachment bond:

"I'm important, valuable, lovable. I can change any behavior that's a problem for us."

"You're important, valuable, lovable. I'll support you while you change any behavior that's a problem for us."

Worksheet 10.11

Homework Assignment # 18
Consolidating Gains

You have learned a deeper understanding of your internal experience—of your thoughts, feelings, behavior, goals, and motivations. You have learned a deeper level of communicating. Now it's crucial to consolidate your gains, to make them a part of yourself, by continuing to practice the skills you have learned.

Write what you have gained from this therapeutic experience. Then recite your list aloud—it's important that you hear your voice consolidating your gains.

Worksheet 10.12

Bite of the Vampire

The emotional pain of attachment abuse works like the *bite of the vampire*—once we get the fangs, we *always* have them and will always be visited by a recurring impulse to make others like ourselves. *Relapse* is forgetting that we have the fangs or forgetting that we can and must keep them retracted.

WARNING SIGNS THAT THE FANGS ARE INCHING FORWARD

irritability

restlessness

moodiness

trouble sleeping

isolation (don't want to go out or see friends or don't want your family to do so)

feeling chilly, closed off

getting angry in traffic

jealousy/envy

feeling an urge to control or spy on family members:

discouraging them from having friends
making them tell you their every move
listening to their phone calls
reading their mail

Worksheet 10.13

Final Homework Assignment # 19 The Healing Letters

Putting the past behind you requires closure, a way of formally drawing a line between the past you, controlled by anger and hurt, and the present you, in control, competent, growth-oriented, compassionate, healing.

THE POWER OF APOLOGY

- closes the past
- opens the future
- forges your identity as *competent, growth-oriented, compassionate, healing.*

Formally writing out the apology is important, whether or not you actually send it.

Form of the written apology

State:

1. *why* you hurt your spouse, children, and parents
   a. what were your intentions
   b. what were you feeling
2. what effects you believe your behavior had on them
3. what effects your hurtful behavior has had on you
4. how much you regret hurting them
5. that understanding yourself has given you the power of self-control
6. specifically what you need to do to keep the fangs retracted in the future.

This is an exercise in *pride* in your entire, ever-growing, complex Self. It shows the difference between what you were in the past and what you have become in the present.

Create the healing letters to serve as documents that you can read regularly for inspiration, to demonstrate clearly the difference between the past you, trapped in the weak modes of self, and the present and future self dominated by the solid integration of your power modes: competent, creative, growth-oriented, healing, nurturing, and compassionate.

Note: This is an exercise in healing, not in hurtful blame. (Blame is about causes and powerlessness; responsibility is about solutions and power.) Don't attempt to justify whatever hurt you did, for that will serve to keep open your wounds. (Don't say, "I only hurt you because you hurt me." Healing means you have learned that you don't *have to* hurt a loved one back, that hurting back only hurts you more.)

Worksheet 10.14

Strategies for Preventing Relapse

- Rehearse *H*EALS often!
- Do the Self-Esteem Transfusion Schedule at least 10 consecutive days.
- Do the Building Immunity to Core Hurts exercise.
- Do the written Conversion Exercise.
- Call a friend or a group member or the group leader.
- Form Compassion Workshop support groups.
- Exercise well.
- Eat well:
    - □ avoid substances that stimulate anxiety or depression, such as caffeine, nicotine, drugs and alcohol, excessive salt, sugar, and preservatives;
    - □ take vitamin supplements, particularly B and C.
- Do something nice for yourself.
- Do something nice for loved ones.

Epilogue

> My father sat still, looking down at his thin lap, as if he'd expected this question all my adult life. It was near the end of his long illness; I could no longer avoid confronting him about the blood my mother shed and the terror she endured throughout their 11-year marriage. I had to ask *why*, because I always knew that he loved my mother and me. His eyes wouldn't move from his lap. I could scarcely recognize his sullen countenance. (He had grown proud of me over the years and always seemed to smile in gratitude for my brief and infrequent visits.) After a long silence, he looked up, but not quite into my eyes. "I know now what part of the reason was," he said slowly. "It was so you would see why you shouldn't be like me."

This book has argued that the extreme form of attachment abuse, family violence, like the mildest forms, results from desperate attachment that, in the absence of self-compassion, gives way to self-loathing. Extreme abusers use the analgesic and amphetamine effects of anger arousal to numb pain, quell anxiety, and temporarily fill the internal power void created by their diminished capacity to love and be loved, to feel compassion and to accept the compassion of others. Their loved ones become the objects of this anger because attachment relationships serve as a kind of mirror image of the loving and lovable self; attachment abusers succumb to the illusion that they might control painful reflections of self by forcefully manipulating the mirror. A new treatment, the Compassion Workshop, attempts to loosen the gaze of attachment abusers from the mirror reflections of their innermost doubts, and direct it, at last, deeply into the hearts of their loved ones. Only then can they learn that, to understand deeply the hurt of another, is to heal one's own.

References

Ainsworth, M. D. S., Blehar, M. C., Waters, E. & Wall, S. (1978). *Patterns of attachment: A psychological study of the strange situation.* Hillsdale, NJ: Erlbaum.

Ainsworth, M. D. S. (1985). I. Patterns of infant-mother attachment: Antecedents and effects on development, and, II. Attachments across the life-span. *Bulletin of the New York Academy of Medicine, 61,* 771–812.

Ainsworth, M. D. S. (1989). Attachments beyond intimacy. *American Psychologist, 34,* 932–937.

Alexander, P. C. (1992). Application of attachment theory to the study of sexual abuse. *Journal of Consulting and Clinical Psychology, 60,* 185–195.

Allan, G. (1988). Kinship: Responsibility and care for elderly people. *Aging and Society, 8,* 294–368.

Allen, C. M., & Straus, M. A. (1979). Resources, power, and husband-wife violence. In M. A. Straus & G. T. Hotaling (Eds.), *The social causes of husband-wife violence* (pp.188–208). Minneapolis: University of Minnesota Press.

Allen, K., Calsyn, D. A., Fehrenbach, P. A., & Benton, G. (1989). A study of interpersonal behaviors of male batterers. *Journal of Interpersonal Violence, 4* 79–89.

Averill, J. R. (1982). *Anger and aggression: An essay on emotion.* New York: Springer Publishing Co.

Archer, J. (Ed.) (1994). *Male violence.* London: Routledge

Ballard, M. E. (1992). *Cardiovascular and psychological responses* to adult's angry behavior in children of hypertensive and non-hypertensive parents. Dissertation Abstracts International.

Barnett, O. W., & Hamberger, L. K. (1992). The assessment of maritally violent men on the California psychological inventory. *Violence and Victims, 7*(1), 15–28.

Barnett, O. W. & Planeaux, P. S. (1989, January). *A hostility-guilt assessment of counseled and uncounseled batterers.* Paper presented at the response to Family Violence Research Conference, Purdue University, West Lafayette, IN.

Baron, R. A. (1976). The reduction of human aggression: A field study of the influence of incompatible responses. *Journal of Applied Social Psychology, 6,* 260–274.

Baron, R. A. (1979). Aggression, empathy, and race: Effects of victim's pain cues, victim's race, and level of instigation on physical aggression. *Journal of Applied Social Psychology, 9,* 103–114.

Baron, R. A. (1983). The control of human aggression: An optimistic overview. *Journal of Social and Clinical Psychology, 1,* 97–119.

Baron, R. A. (1984). Reducing organizational conflict: An incompatible response approach. *Journal of Applied Psychology, 69,* 272–279.

Bartholomew, K., & Horowitz, L. M. (1991). Attachment styles among young adults: A test of a four-category model. *Journal of Personality and Social Psychology, 61,* 226–244.

Baumeister, R. F. (1991). *Meanings of life.* New York: Guilford Press.

Baumeister, R. F. (1992, August). *Self-regulation.* Paper presented to the annual meeting of the American Psychological Association, Washington, DC.

Baumeister, R. F., Stillwell, A. M., & Heatherton, T. F. (1994). Guilt: An interpersonal approach. *Psychological Bulletin, 115,* 243–267.

Beck, A. T. (1976). *Cognitive therapy and the emotional disorders.* New York: New American Library.

Beck, A. T., Rush, A. J., Shaw, B. F., & Emery, G. (1979). *Cognitive therapy of depression.* New York: Guilford.

Belenky, M. F., Clinchy, B. M., Goldberger, N. R., & Tarule, J. M. (1986). *Women's ways of knowing: The development of self, voice, and mind.* New York: Basic Books.

Bell, S. M., & Ainsworth, M. D. S. (1972). Infant crying and maternal responsiveness. *Child Development, 43,* 1171–1190.

Berk, L. E. (1989). *Child development.* Boston: Allyn and Bacon.

Berkowitz, L. (1990). On the formation and regulation of anger and aggression: A cognitive-neoassociationistic analysis. *American Psychologist, 45,* 494–503.

Berkowitz, L., & Heimer, K. (1989). On the construction of the anger experience: Aversive events and negative priming in the formation of feelings. *Advances in Experimental Social Psychology, 22,* 1–37.

Biaggio, M. K. (1987). Clinical dimensions of anger management. *American Journal of Psychotherapy, 16,* 417–427.

Bograd, M. (1988). Feminist perspectives on wife abuse: An introduction. In K. Yllo & M. Bograd (Eds). *Feminist perspectives on wife abuse* (pp. 11–26). Newbury Park, CA: Sage.

Bonnett, K. S., Miller, J. M., & Simon, E. J. (1976). The effects of chronic opiate treatment and social isolation on opiate receptors in the rodent brain. In H. W. Kosterlitz (Ed). *Opiate and endogenous opioid peptides.* Amsterdam: Elsevier.

Boulton, M. J. (1994). The relationship between playful and aggressive fighting in children, adolescents and adults. In J. Archer (Ed.), *Male violence* (pp. 23–41). London: Routledge.

Bowker, L. (1983). *Beating wife beating.* Lexington, MA: D. C. Heath.

Bowlby, J. (1969). *Attachment and loss, Vol. I: Attachment.* New York: Basic Books.

Bowlby, J. (1973). *Attachment and loss, Vol. II: Separation: Anxiety and anger.* New York: Basic Books.

Bowlby, J. (1977). The making and breaking of affectional bonds: I. Etiology and psychopathology in the light of attachment theory. *British Journal of Psychiatry, 130,* 201–210.

Bowlby, J. (1980). *Attachment and loss, Vol. III: Loss, depression and sadness.* New York: Basic Books.

Bowlby, J. (1984). Violence in the family as a disorder of the attachment and caregiving systems. *The American Journal of Psychoanalysis, 44*(1), 9–27.

Bowlby, J. (1988). *Clinical applications of attachment: A secure base.* London: Routledge.

Brazelton, T. B., Koslowski, B., & Main, M. (1974). The origins of reciprocity: The early mother-infant interaction. In M. Lewis & L. A. Rosenblum (Eds.) *The effect of the infant on its caregivers.* New York: Wiley.

Bretherton, I. (1985). Attachment theory: Retrospect and prospect. In I. Bretherton & E. Waters (Eds.), Growing points in attachment theory and research. *Monographs of the Society for Research in Child Development, 50* (1–2 Serial No. 209), 3–35.

Broadbent, D. E. (1971). *Decision and stress.* San Diego, CA: Academic Press.

Broucek, F. J. (1991). *Shame and the self.* New York: Guilford.

Bureau of Justice Statistics. (1988). Department of Justice: Washington, DC.

Bush, H., Shaw, S., Cleary, P., Delbanco, T. L., & Aronson, M. D. (1987). Screening for alcohol abuse using the CAGE questionnaire. *The American Journal of Medicine, 82* 231–235.

Cahn, T. S. (1988). *Stress, social suport and anger in domestically violent men.* UMI Dissertation Abstracts.

Cassidy, J. (1988). Child-mother attachment and the self in six year-olds. *Child Development, 59,* 121–134.

Claes, J. A. & Rosenthal, D. M. (1990). Men who batter women: A study in power. *Journal of Family Violence, 5,* 215–224.

Collins, N. L. & Read, S. J. (1990). Adult attachment, working models, and relationship quality in dating couples. *Journal of Personality and Social Psychology, 38,* 644–643.

Condry, J., & Condry, S. (1976). Sex differences: A study of the eye of the beholder. *Child Development, 4,* 812–819.

Conner, K. R., & Ackerley, G. D. (1994). Alcohol-related battering: Developing treatment strategies. *Journal of Family Violence, 9,*143–155.

Conte, J. (1985). Clinical dimensions of adult sexual interest in children. *Behavioral Sciences and the Law, 3,* 341–354.

Crawford, M., & Gartner, R. (1992). *Women killing: Intimate femicide in Ontario, 1974–1990.* Women's Directorate, Ministry of Social Services, Toronto, Ontario.

Cribb, D. A., Ozone, S. J., & Pipes, F. (1992, August). A compilation of personality instruments. Paper presented to the Annual Meeting of the American Psychological Association, Washington, D C.

Crowell, J. A., & Feldman, S. S. (1987). Mothers' internal models of relationships and children's behavioral and developmental status: A study of mother-child interactions. *Child Development, 59,* 1273–1285.

da Gloria, J. (1984). Frustration, aggression, and the sense of justice. In A. Mummendey (Ed), *Social psychology and aggression: From individual behavior to social interaction* (pp. 127–142). New York: Springer Publishing Co.

Daldrup, R. J., Beutler, L. E., Engle, D., & Greenberg, L. S. (1988). *Focused expressive psychotherapy: Freeing the overcontrolled patient.* New York: The Guilford Press.

Daly, M., & Wilson, M. (1988). *Homicide.* New York: Aldine De Gruyter.

Dankwort, J. (1991). Research goals and designs: Reflections on studies regarding intervention with wife abusers. In R. K. Hanson & L. Hart (Eds.), *The evaluation of treatment programs for male batterers* (pp. 37–58). Conference proceedings: Ministry of the Solicitor General of Canada.

Davidson, J. (1978). *Conjugal crime.* New York: Hawthorne Books.

DeLozier, P. P. (1982). Attachment theory and child abuse. In C. M. Parkes & J. Stevenson-Hinde (Eds.) *The place of attachment in human behavior* (pp. 95–117). New York: Basic Books.

Demo, D. H. (1985). The measurement of self-esteem: Refining our methods. *Journal of Personality and Social Psychology, 48,* 1490–1502.

Diamond, E. L. (1982). The role of anger and hostility in essential hypertension and coronary heart diesease. *Psychological Bulletin, 92,* 410–433.

Dobson, K. S., & Block, L. (1988). Historical and philosophical bases of the cognitive-behavioral therapies. In K. S. Dobson (Eds), *Handbook of cognitive-behavioral therapies* (pp. 3–38). New York: The Guilford Press.

Dodge, K. A. (1991). Emotion and social information processing. In J. Garber & K. A. Dodge (Eds.), *The development of emotion regulation and dysregulation* (pp. 159–181). Cambridge, UK: Cambridge University Press.

Dodge, K. A., & Coie, J. D. (1987). Social-information-processing factors in reactive and proactive aggression in children's peer groups. *Journal of Personality and Social Psychology, 53,* 1146–1158.

Dodge, K. A., & Frame, C. M. (1982). Social cognitive biases and deficits in aggressive boys. *Child Development, 53,* 620–635.

Dodge, K. A., & Newman, J. P. (1981). Biased decision making processes in aggressive boys. *Journal of Abnormal Psychology, 90,* 375–379.

Dodge, K. A., Pettit, G. S., McClaskey, C. L., & Brown, M. M. (1986). Social competence in children. *Monographs for the Society for Research in Child Development, 51,* 213–224.

Dodge, K. A., & Tomlin, A. (1987). Cue-utilization as a mechanism of bias in aggressive children. *Social Cognition, 5*, 280–300.

Dunn, J., & Brown, J. (1991). Relationships, talk about feelings, and the development of affect regulation in early childhood. In J. Garber & K. A. Dodge (Eds.), *The development of emotion regulation and dysregulation* (pp. 89–108). Cambridge, UK: Cambridge University Press.

Dutton, D. G. (1986). The outcome of court-mandated treatment for wife-assault: A quasi-experimental evaluation. *Violence and Victims, 1*, 163–175.

Dutton, D. G. (1988). *The domestic assault of women.* Newton, MA: Allyn and Bacon.

Dutton, D. G. (1994). Behavioral and affective correlates of Borderline Personality Organization in wife assaulters. *International Journal of Criminial Justice and Behavior, 17*(3), 26–38.

Dutton, D. G. (1994). Patriarchy and wife assault: The ecological fallacy. *Violence and Victims, 9*, 167–182.

Dutton, D. G., & Browning, J. J. (1988). Concern for power, fear of intimacy, and aversive stimuli for wife abuse. In G. T. Hotaling, D. Finkelhor, J. T. Kilpatric, & M. A. Straus (Eds.), *New directions in family violence research* (pp 163–175). Newbury Park, CA: Sage.

Dutton, D. G., Saunders, K., Starzomski, A. & Bartholomew, K. (1994). Intimacy-anger and insecure attachment as precursors of abuse in intimate relationships. *Journal of Applied Social Psychology, 24*, 1367–1368.

Dutton, D. G., & Strachan, C. E. (1987). Motivational needs for power and spouse-specific assertiveness in assaultive and nonassaultive men. *Violence and Victims, 2*, 145–156.

Easterbrook, J. A. (1959). The effects of emotion on cue utilization and the organization of behavior. *Psychological Review, 66*, 183–201.

Egeland, B. Jacobvitz, D., & Sroufe, L. A. (1988). Breaking the cycle of abuse. *Child Development, 59*, 1080–1088.

Egeland, B. & Sroufe, L. A. (1981). Attachment and early maltreatment. *Child Development, 52*, 44–52.

Eisenberg, N., & Mussen, P. H. (1989). *The roots of prosocial behavior in children.* New York: Cambridge University Press.

Eisikovits, Z. C., & Edleson, J. L. (1989). Intervening with men who batter: A critical review of the literature. *Social Service Review*, 384–414.

Eisikovits, Z. C., Edleson, J. L., Guttmann, E., & Sela-Amit, M.

(1991). Cognitive styles and socialized attitudes of men who batter: Where should we intervene? *Family Relations, 40,* 72–77.

Ellis, A. (1985). *Overcoming resistance: Rational-emotive therapy with difficult clients.* New York: Springer Publishing Co.

Epstein, S. (1979). The ecological study of emotions in humans. In P. Pliner, K. R. Blankstein, & I. M. Spigel (Eds.) *Perceptions of emotion in self and others.* New York: Plenum Press.

Eron, L. D., & Huesmann, L. R. (1989). The genesis of gender differences in aggression. In M. A. Luszcz & T. Nettelbeck (Eds.), *Psychological development: Perspectives across the life-span.* North-Holland: Elsevier Science.

Eron, L. D., Walder, L. O., Huesmann, L. R., & Lefkowitz, M. M. (1974). The convergence of laboratory and field studies of the development of aggression. In J. deWitt & W. W. Hartup (Eds.), *Determinants and origins of aggressive behavior* (pp. 347–380). The Hague: Mouten.

Ewing, J. A. (1984). Detecting alcoholism: The CAGE questionnaire. *Journal of the American Medical Association, 252,* 1906–1907.

Ewing, J. A., & Rouse, B. A. (1970, February). *Identifying the hidden alcoholic.* Paper presented at the 29th International Conference on Alcohol and Drug Dependence.

Eysenck, M. W. (1976). Arousal, learning, and memory. *Psychological Bulletin, 83,* 389–404.

Eysenck, M. W. (1982). *Attention and arousal.* New York: Springer Publishing Co.

Fagot, B. I. (1978). The influence of sex of child on parental reactions to toddler children. *Child Development, 49,* 459–465.

Feeny, J. A., & Noller, P. (1990). Attachment style as predictor of adult romantic relationships. *Journal of Personality and Social Psychology, 58,* 281–291.

Feshbach, S. (1970). Aggression. In P. H. Mussen (Ed.), *Carmichael's manual of child psychology* (Vol 2., pp. 159–259). New York: Wiley.

Field, T. (1985). Attachment as psychobiological attunement: Being on the same wavelength. In M. Reite & T. Field (Eds.), *The psychobiology of attachment and separation* (pp. 415–454). Orlando: Academic Press.

Firestone, R. W. (1990). *Compassionate child-rearing: An in-depth approach to optimal parenting.* New York: Plenum.

Fischer, J. L. (1981). Transitions in relationship style from adolescence to young adulthood. *Journal of Youth and Adolescence, 10,* 11–23.

Fish, B. (1993). Meaning and attachment in mothers and toddlers. *Child and Adolescent Social Work Journal 10* (3), 177–188.

Flournoy, P. S. & Wilson, G. L. (1991). Brief research report: Assessment of MMPI profiles of male batterers. *Violence and Victims, 6,* 309–320.

Follingstad, D. R., Rutledge, L. L. Berg, B. J. Hause, E. S., & Polek, D. S. (1990). The role of emotional abuse in physically abusive relationships. *Journal of Family Violence, 5,* 107–120.

Frisch, H. L. (1977). Sex stereotypes in adult-infant play. *Child Development, 48,* 1671–1675.

Ganley, A. L., & Harris, L. (August, 1978). *Domestic violence issues in designing and implementing programs for male batterers.* American Psychological Association, Toronto, Ontario.

Garcia, J. L., & Kosberg, J. I. (1992). Understanding anger: Implications for formal and informal caregivers. *Journal of Elder Abuse & Neglect,* 4(4), 87–99.

Gardner, A. (1993, August). *Insecure attachment in women at high risk: Correlations to abandonment and abuse in childhood.* Paper presented at the annual convention of the American Psychological Association, Toronto, Ontario.

Geffner, R. A. & Rosenbaum, A. (1990). Characteristics and treatment of batterers. *Behavioral Sciences and the Law, 8,* 131–140.

Gelles, R. J. (1974). *The violent home: A study of physical aggression between husbands and wives.* Newbury Park, CA: Sage.

Gelles, R. J. (1975). Violence and pregnancy: A note on the extent of the problem and needed services. *Family Coordinator, 24,* 81–86.

Gelles, R. J. & Cornell, C. P. (1990). *Intimate violence in families* (2nd ed). Newbury Park, CA: Sage.

Gelles, R. J., & Harrop, J. W. (1989). Violence, battering, and psychological distress among women. *Journal of Interpersonal Violence, 4,* 400–420.

Gilbert, P. (1989). *Human nature and suffering.* London: Erlbaum.

Gilbert, P. (1992). *Depression: The evolution of powerlessness.* New York: Guilford.

Gilbert, P. (1994). Male violence: Toward an integration. In J. Archer (Ed.), *Male violence.* London: Routledge.

Goldstein, D., & Rosenbaum, A. (1985). An evaluation of the self-esteem of maritally violent men. *Family Relations, 34,* 425–428.

Gondolf, E. W. (1985). Anger and oppression in men who batter: Empiricist and feminist perspectives and their implications for research. *Victimology: An International Journal, 10,* 311–324.

Gondolf, E. W. (1987). Changing men who batter: A developmental model for integrated interventions. *Journal of Family Violence, 2,* 335–349.

Gondolf, E. W. (1988). Who are those guys? Toward a behavioral typology of batterers. *Violence and Victims, 3,* 187–203.

Greenblat, C. S. (1985). "Don't hit your wife...unless": Preliminary findings on normative support for the use of physical force by husbands. *Victimology: An International Journal, 10,* 221–241.

Greer, S. & Morris, T. (1975). Psychological attributes of women who develop breast cancer: A controlled study. *Journal of Psychosomatic Research, 2,* 147–153.

Grossmann, K., Grossmann, K. E., Huber, F., & Wartner, U. (1981). German children's behavior toward their mothers at 12 months and their fathers at 18 months in Ainsworth's Strange Situation. *International Journal of Behavioral Development, 4,* 157–181.

Grossmann, K., Fremmer-Bombik, E., Rudolf, J., & Grossmann, K. E. (1988). Maternal attachment representations as related to patterns of infant-mother attachment and maternal care during the first year. In R. A. Hinde & J. Stevenson-Hinde (Eds.), *Relationships within families* (pp. 241–260). Oxford, England: Clarendon Press.

Guidano, V. F. (1987). *The complexity of self.* New York: The Guilford Press.

Guidano, V. F. (1991). *The self in process.* New York: The Guilford Press.

Guidano, V. F., & Liotti, G. (1983). *Cognitive processes and emotional disorders.* New York: The Guilford Press.

Hale, G., Duckworth, J., Zimostrad, S., & Nichols, D. (1988). Abusive partners: MMPI profiles of male batterers. *Journal of Mental Health Counseling, 10* 214–224.

Hamberger, L. K., & Hastings, J. (1988a). Characteristics of male spouse abusers consistent with personality disorders. *Hospital and Community Psychiatry, 39,* 763–770.

Hamberger, L. K., & Hastings, J. (1988b). Skills training for treatment of spouse abusers: An outcome study. *Journal of Family Violence, 3*, 121–130.

Harlow, H. F. & Zimmerman, R. R. (1959). Affectional responses in infant monkeys. *Science, 130* 421.

Harman, J. I. (1985). Relations among components of the empathic process. *Journal of Counseling Psychology, 33*, 371–376.

Harris, M. B. (1992). Beliefs about how to reduce anger. *Psychological Reports, 70*, 203–210.

Hart, S. D., Dutton, D. G., & Nevlove, T. (1994). The prevalence of personality disorder among wife assaulters. *Journal of Personality Disorders, 7*, 329–341.

Hazan, C. & Huth, M. J. (1993). *Continuity and change in inner working models of attachment.* Unpublished manuscript.

Hazan, C., & Shaver, P. (1987). Conceptualizing romantic love as an attachment process. *Journal of Personality and Social Psychology, 52*, 511–524.

Hilberman, E. & Munson, K. (1977–78). Sixty battered women. *Victimology: An International Journal, 2*, 460–470.

Hindy, C. G., & Schwarz, J. C. (1994). Anxious romantic attachment in adult relationships. In M. S. Sperling & W. H. Berman (Eds.), *Attachment in Adults: Clinical and developmental perspectives* (pp. 179–203). New York: Guilford.

Hogan, R. T. (1969). Development of an empathy scale. *Journal of Consulting and Clinical Psychology, 33*, 307–316.

Holtzworth-Munroe, A. (1988). Causal attributions in marital violence: Theoretical and methodological issues. *Clinical Psychology Review, 8*, 331–344.

Holtzworth-Munroe, A. (1992). Attributions and maritally violent men: The role of cognitions in marital violence. In J. H. Harvey, T. H. Orbuch, & A. L. Weber (Eds.), *Attributions, accounts, and close relationships* (pp. 165–175). New York: Springer Publishing Co.

Holtzworth-Munroe, A. & Hutchinson, G. (1993). Attributing negative intent to wife behavior: The attributions of maritally violent versus nonviolent men. *Journal of Abnormal Psychology, 102*, 206–211.

Izard, C. E., & Schwartz, G. M. (1986). Patterns of emotion in depression. In M. Rutter, C. Izard & P. Read (Eds.), *Depression in young people: Developmental and clinical perspectives* (pp. 33–70). New York: Guilford.

Jacobson, N., & Gottman, J. M. (1993, August). Vagal reactors. Paper presented to the annual meeting of the American Psychological Association, Toronto, Ontario.

Janoff-Bulman, R. & Frieze, I. H. (1983). A theoretical perspective for understanding reactions to victimization. *Journal of Social Issues, 39,* 1–17.

Joseph, R. A., Markus, H. R., & Tafarodi, R. W. (1992). Gender and self-esteem. *Journal of Personality and Social Psychology, 63,* 391–403.

Julian, T. W., & McKenry, P. C. (1993). Mediators of male violence toward female intimates. *Journal of Family Violence, 8,* 39–55.

Kagan, J. (1989). *Unstable ideas: Temperament, cognition, and self.* Cambridge, MA: Harvard University Press.

Kaplan, N., & Main, M. (1985, April). Internal representations of attachment at six years as indicated by family drawings and verbal response to imagined separations. In M. Main (Chair), *Attachment: A move to the level of represenation.* Symposium at the meeting of the Society for Research in Child Development, Toronto, Ontario.

Kashani, J. H., Daniel, A. E., Dandoy, A. C., & Holcomb, W. R. (1992). Family violence: Impact on children. *Journal of the American Academy of Child and Adolescent Psychiatry, 31,* 181–189.

Katsikas, S., Petretic-Jackson, P., Betz, W., Ames, D., Pitman, L., & Lawless, M. (1993, August). *Childhood abuse predicts adult trauma symptomatology: An attachment perspective.* Paper presented at the annual convention of the American Psychological Association, Toronto, Ontario.

Katz, J. (1988). *Seductions to crime.* New York: Basic Books.

Kegan, R. (1982). *The evolving self: Problem and process in human development.* Cambridge, MA: Harvard University Press.

Kellner, R. (1987). A symptom questionnaire. *Journal of Clinical Psychiatry, 48,* 268–274.

Kernis, M. H., Grannemann, B. D., & Barclay, L. C. (1989). Stability and level of self-esteem as predictors of anger arousal and hostility. *Journal of Personality and Social Psychology, 56,* 1013–1022.

Kiecolt-Glaser, J. K., Fisher, L. D., Ogrocki, B. S., Stout, J. C., Carl, B. S., Speicher, M. D., & Glaser, R. (1987). Marital quality, marital disruption and immune function. *Psychosomatic Medicine, 49,* 13–34.

Klinnert, M. D., & Bingham, R. D. (1994). The organizing effects of early relationships. *Psychiatry: Interpersonal and Biological Processes, 57*(1), 1–10.

Kobak, R. R., & Sceery, A. (1988). Attachment in late adolescence: Working models, affect regulation, and representation of self and others. *Child Development, 59,* 135–146.

Kohlberg, L. (1981). *The philosophy of moral development.* San Francisco: Harper & Row.

Lansky, M. (1987). Shame and domestic violence. In D. L. Nathanson (Ed.), *The many faces of shame* (pp. 335–362) New York: The Guilford Press.

Lau, E., & Kosberg, J. (1979). Abuse of the elderly by informal care providers. *Aging, 299,* 10–15.

Leonard, K. E., Brommet, E. J., Parkinson, D. K., Day, N. L. & Ryan, C. M. (1985). Patterns of alcohol abuse and physically aggressive behavior in men. *Journal of Studies on Alcohol. 46*(4), 279–282.

Levant, R. F. (1992). Toward the reconstruction of masculinity. *Journal of Family Psychology, 5,* 379–402.

Levenson, M. R. (1992). Rethinking psychopathy. *Theory and Psychology, 2,* 51–71.

Lever, J. (1976). Sex differences in the games children play. *Social Work, 23*(4), 78–87.

Levine, J. D., Gordon, N. C., & Fields, H. (1978). The mechanism of placebo analgesia. *The Lancet, September 23,* 654–657.

Lewis, H. B. (1971). Shame and guilt in neurosis. *The Psychoanalytic Review, 58,* 434–435.

Lewis, H. B. (1976). *Psychic war in men and women.* New York: New York University Press.

Lewis, H. B. (Ed.), (1989). *The role of shame in symptom formation.* Hillsdale, NJ: Erlbaum.

Lewis, W. A., & Bucher, A. M. (1992). Anger, catharsis, the reformulated frustration-aggression hypothesis, and health consequences. *Psychotherapy, 29,* 385–392.

Litman, G., Eiser, J., Rawson, N., & Oppenheim, A. (1979). Differences in relapse precipitants and coping behaviors between alcohol relapsers and survivors. *Behavioral Research and Therapy, 17,* 89–94.

Lorenz, K. Z. (1963). *On aggression.* New York: Harcourt, Brace and World.

Lyddon, W. J., & Alford, D. J. (1993). Constructivist assessment: A developmental-epistemic perspective. In G. J. Neimeyer (Ed.),

Constructivist assessment: A casebook (pp. 31–57). Newbury Park, CA: Sage.

Lynch, J. J. (1990). The broken heart: The psychobiology of human contact. In R. Ornstein & C. Swencionis (Eds.), *The healing brain: A scientific reader.* New York: Guilford Press.

Maccoby, E. E. (1990). Gender and relationships: A developmental account. *American Psychologist, 45,* 513–520.

MacDonald, K. B. (1988). *Social and personality development: An evolutionary synthesis.* New York: Plenum Press.

McAdams, D. P. (1988). Personal needs and personal relationships. In S. Duck (Ed.), *Handbook of personal relationships: Theory, research and interventions* (pp. 7–22). New York: Wiley.

McMahon, C. E. & Sheikh, A. A. (1984). Imagination in disease healing processes: A historical perspective. In A. A. Sheikh (Ed.), *Imagination and healing* (pp. 7–34). Farmingdale, NY: Bayward Publishing Company, Inc.

Maiuro, R. D., Cahn, T. S., & Vitaliano, P. P. (1986). Assertiveness deficits and hostility in domestically violent men. *Violence and Victims, 1,* 279–289.

Maiuro, R. D., Cahn, T. S. Vitaliano, P. P., Wagner, B. C. & Zegree, J. B. (1988). Anger, hostility, and depression in domestically violent versus generally assaultive men and nonviolent control subjects. *Journal of Consulting and Clinical Psychology, 56*(1), 17–23.

Main, M., & Goldwyn, R. (1984). Predicting rejection of her infant from mother's representation of her own experience: Implications for the abused-abusing intergenerational cycle. *Child Abuse & Neglect, 8,* 203–217.

Main, M., Kaplan, N., & Cassidy, J. (1985). Security in infancy, childhood, and adulthood: A move toward the level of representation. *Monographs of the Society for Research in Child Development, 50*(1–2), 66–104.

Margolin, G., John, R., & Gleberman, L. (1988). Affective response to conflictual discussion in violent and nonviolent couples. *Journal of Consulting and Clinical Psychology, 56,* 24–33.

Marlatt, G., & Gordon, J. (Eds), (1985). *Relapse prevention.* New York: Guilford Press.

Marshall, W. L., Laws, D. R., &Barbaree, H. E. (Eds.) (1990). *Handbook of sexual assault: Issues, theories, and treatment of the offender.* New York: Plenum Press.

Martin, D. (1976). *Battered wives of America.* San Francisco: Glide.

Masters, W. L. (1993, August). Sex therapy: Past, present, future. Paper presented at the Annual Meeting of the American Psychological Association, Toronto, Ontario.

Mayfield, D., McLeod, G., & Hall, P. (1974). The CAGE questionnaire: Validation of a new alcoholism screening instrument. *American Journal of Psychiatry, 131,* 1121–1122.

Meichenbaum, D. (1977). *Cognitive behavioral modification: An integrative approach.* New York: Plenum.

Miedzian, M. (1992). *Boys will be boys: Breaking the link between masculinity and violence.* London: Virago

Miller, J. B. (1986). *Toward a new psychology of women* (2nd ed.). Boston: Beacon Press.

Miller, P. A., & Eisenberg, N. (1988). The relation of empathy to aggressive behavior and externalising/antisocial behavior. *Psychological Bulletin, 103,* 324–344.

Morris, D. (1981). Attachment and intimacy. In G. Stricker (Ed.), *Intimacy* (pp. 305–323). New York: Plenum.

Murphy, C. (1991). *Sex role strain, emotional vulnerability, and wife abuse.* Ann Arbor, MI: UMI Dissertation Information Service.

Murphy, C., Scott, E., Meyer, S., & O'Leary, K. D. (1992). Emotional vulnerability patterns in partner assaultive men. Paper submitted as part of a symposium for the 1992 AABT convention.

Nathanson, D. L. (1992). *Shame and pride: Affect, sex, and the birth of the self.* New York: W. W. Norton.

National Institute of Justice. (1983). *Non-stranger violence: The criminal court's response.* Washington, DC: U. S. Department of Justice.

Neidig, P. H. (1991). *Domestic conflict containment program workbook (Revised Edition).* Beaufort, SC: Behavioral Science Associates.

Neidig, P. H., Friedman, D. H., & Collins, B. S. (1986). Attitudinal characteristics of males who have engaged in spouse abuse. *Journal of Family Violence, 1,* 223–233.

Neidigh, L., Gesten, E. & Shiffman, G. (1988). Coping with the temptation to drink. *Addictive Behaviors, 13,* 1–9. Neidigh, L. & Tomiko, R. (1991). The coping strategies of child sexual abusers. *Journal of Sex Education and Therapy, 17,* 103–110.

Newman, J. D., Murphy, M. R., & Harbough, C. R. (1982). Naloxone-reversible suppression of isolation call production after morphine injections in squirrel monkeys. *Social Neuroscience Abstract, 8,* 940.

Notarius, C. I., & Herrick, L. R. (1989). The psychophysiology of dyadic interaction. In H. Wagner & A. Manstead (Eds.), *Handbook of social psychophysiology.* New York: Wiley.

Novaco, R. W. (1975). *Anger control: The development and evaluation of an experimental treatment.* Lexington, MA: Heath.

Ornstein, R., & Sobel, D. S. (1987). *The healing brain.* New York: Touchstone.

Ornstein, R., & Sobel, D. S. (1990). The brain as a health maintenance organization. In R. Ornstein & C. Swencionis (Eds.), *The healing brain: A scientific reader.* New York: Guilford Press.

Osborne, R. W. (1991). Men and intimacy: An empirical review. In R. Levant, Chair, *Men, emotions, and intimacy.* Symposium conducted at the Annual Meeting of the American Psychological Association, San Francisco.

Overholser, J., & Beck, S. (1986). Multimethod assessment of rapists, child molesters and three control groups on behavioral and psychological measures. *Journal of Consulting and Clinicial Psychology, 54,* 682–687.

Pagelow, M. (1981). *Women battering: Victims and their experiences.* Newbury Park, CA: Sage.

Panksepp, J. (1982). Toward a general psychobiological theory of emotions. *Behavior Brain Science, 5,* 407–468.

Panksepp, J. (1989). The neurobiology of emotions: Of animal brains and human feelings. In H. Wagner & A. Manstead (Eds.), *Handbook of social psychophysiology* (pp. 5–25). New York: John Wiley & Sons.

Panksepp, J., Najam, N. & Soares, F. (1979). Morphine reduces social cohesion in rats. *Pharmacological Biochemistry Behavior, 11,* 131–134.

Panksepp, J., Sivey, S. M., & Normansell, L. A. (1985). Brain opioids and social emotions. In M. Reite & T. Fields (Eds.), *The psychobiology of attachment and separation.* Orlando: Academic Press.

Pence, E., & Paymar, M. (1993). *Education groups for men who batter: The Duluth model.* New York: Springer Publishing Co.

Piaget, J. (1932/1965). *The moral development of the child.* New York: Free Press.

Potter-Efron, R. T., & Potter-Efron, P. S. (1991). *Anger, alcoholism and addiction: Treating individuals, couples, and families.* New York: W. W. Norton.

Redd, W. H., Morris, E. K., & Martin, J. A. (1975). Effects of positive and negative adult-child interaction on children's social preferences. *Journal of Experimental Child Psychology, 19*, 153–164.

Reid, J. B., Kavanagh, K., & Baldwin, D. V. (1987). Abusive parents' perceptions of child problem behaviors: A example of parental bias. *Journal of Abnormal Child Psychology, 15*, 457–466.

Reis, H. T. (1986). Gender effects in social participation: Intimacy, lonelinesss, and the conduct of social interaction. In R. Gilmour & S. Duck (Eds.), *The emerging field of personal relationships* (pp. 91–105).

Retzinger, S. M. (1991a). Shame, anger, and conflict: Case study of emotional violence. *Journal of Family Violence, 6*(1), 37–60.

Retzinger, S. M. (1991b). *Violent emotions: Shame and rage in marital quarrels.* Newbury Park, CA: Sage Publications.

Ricks, M. (1985). The social inheritance of parenting. In I Bretherton & E. Waters (Eds.), Growing points of attachment theory and research. *Monographs of the Society for Research in Child Development, 50* (1-2, Serial No. 209), 211–227.

Rider, M. S. (1985). Entrainment mechanisms are involved in pain reduction, muscle relaxation, and music mediated imagery. *Journal of Music Therapy, 22*(4), 183–192.

Riggs, D. S., Dancu, C. V., Gershuny, B. S., Greenberg, D., & Foa, E. B. (1992). Anger and post-traumatic stress disorder in female crime victims. *Journal of Traumatic Stress, 5*, 613–625.

Rogeness, G. A., Amrung, S. A., Macedo, C. A., Harris, W. R., & Fisher, C. (1986). Psychopathology in abused and neglected children. *Journal of the American Academy of Child Psychiatry, 25*, 659–665.

Rohde, P., Lewinsohn, P. M., Tilson, M., & Seeley, J. R. (1990). Dimensionality of coping and its relation to depression. *Journal of Personality and Social Psychology, 58*, 499–511.

Rosen, I. (1991). Self-esteem as a factor in social and domestic violence. *British Journal of Psychiatry, 158*, 18–23.

Rosenbaum, M. (1980). A schedule for assessing self-control behaviors: Preliminary findings. *Behavior Therapy, 11*, 109–121.

Rosenberg, M. (1965). *Society and the adolescent self-image.* Princeton, NJ: Princeton University Press.

Rosenzweig, S. (1944), An outline of frustration theory. In J. McV. Hunt (Ed.), *Personality and behavior disorders* (pp. 379–388). New York: Ronald Press.

Rothbart, M. K., & Rothbart, M. (1976). Birth order, sex of child, and maternal help giving. *Sex Roles, 2,* 39–46.

Rounsaville, B. J. (1978). Theories of marital violence: Evidence from a study of battered women. *Victimology, 3,* 11–31.

Rouse, L. P. (1984). Models, self-esteem, and locus of control as factors contributing to spouse abuse. *Victimology, 9*(1), 130–141.

Roy, M. (1982). *The abusing partner: An analysis of domestic battering.* New York: Van Nostrand Reinhold Company.

Rule, B. G., & Nesdale, A. R. (1974). Differing functions of aggression. *Journal of Personality, 42,* 467–481.

Russell, D. (1982). The causal dimension scale: A measure of how individuals perceive causes. *Journal of Personality and Social Psychology, 42,* 1137–1145.

Sapiente, A. A. (1988). *Locus of control and causal attributions of maritally violent men.* Unpublished Doctoral Dissertation. California School of Professional Psychology, Los Angeles.

Saunders, D. G. (1987, July). *Are there different types of men who batter? An empirical study with possible implications for treatment.* Paper presented at the meeting of the Third National Family Violence Research Conference, University of New Hampshire, Durham, NH.

Scheff, T. J. (1989). Cognitive and emotional conflict in anorexia: Re-analysis of a case. *Psychiatry, 52,* 148–159.

Scheff, T. J. (1990). *Microsociology: Discourse, emotion, and social structure.* Chicago: University of Chicago Press.

Sheikh, A. A., & Jordan, C. S. (1983). Clinical uses of mental imagery. In A. A. Sheikh (Ed.), *Imagery* (pp. 391–435). New York: Wiley & Sons.

Shields, N. M., & Hanneke, C. R. (1983). Attribution processes in violent relationships: Perceptions of violent husbands and their wives. *Journal of Applied Social Psychology, 13,* 515–527.

Sidorowicz, L. S., & Lunney, G. S. (1980). Baby X Revisited. *Sex Roles, 6,* 67–73.

Slaby, R. G., & Guerra, N. G. (1988). Cognitive mediators of aggression in adolescent offenders: 1. assessment. *Developmental Psychology, 24,* 580–588.

Smail, D. (1987). *Taking care: An aiternative to therapy.* London: J. Dent & Sons.

Sonkin, D. J., & Durphy, M. (1989). *Learning to live without violence: A handbook for men (Updated).* Volcano, CA: Volcano Press.

Sonkin, D. J., Martin, D., & Walker, L. E. (1985). *The male batterer.* New York: Springer Publishing Co.

Sperling, M. B., & Berman, W. H. (Eds.) (1994). *Attachment in adults: Clinical and developmental perspectives.* New York: Guilford Press.

Spitz, R. A. (1945). Hospitalism: An enquiry into the genesis of psychiatric conditions in early childhood. *The Psychoanalytic Study of the Child, 1,* 53–74.

Spitz, R. A. (1946). Anaclitic depression: An inquiry into the genesis of psychiatric conditions in childhood. *The Psychoanalytic Study of the Child, 2,* 313–342.

. Sroufe, L.A. (1984). The organization of emotional development. In K. P. Scherer & P. Ekman (Eds.), *Approaches to emotion* (pp. 109–128). Hillsdale, NJ: Erlbaum.

Sroufe, L.A. (1985). Attachment classification from the perspective of infant-caregiver relationships and infant temperament. *Child Development, 56,* 1–14.

Stark, E., & Flitcraft, A. (1985). Woman-battering, child abuse and social heredity: What is the relationship? In N. Johnson (Ed.), *Marital violence.* Sociological Review Monograph #31. London: Rutledge & Kegan Paul.

Stern, D. (1985). *The interpersonal world of the infant.* New York: Basic Books.

Stordeur, R. A., & Stille, R. (1989). *Ending men's violence against their partners: One road to peace.* Newbury Park, CA: Sage.

Storr, A. (1988). *Human agression.* New York: Bantam.

Stosny, S. (1992, May). *Shadows of the heart: New options in treatment of spouse abusers.* Paper presented at the Maryland Conference of Social Work Practice in Public Mental Health, Marriottsville, Maryland.

Stosny, S. (1993). *The powerful self.* Unpublished manuscript.

Stosny, S. (1994). "Shadows of the heart": A dramatic video for the treatment resistance of spouse abusers. *Social Work, 39,* 686–694.

Straus, M. A. (1979). Measuring intrafamily conflict and violence: The conflict tactic scales. *Journal of Marriage and the Family, 41,* 75–88.

Straus, M. A., & Gelles, R. J. (1988). *Physical violence in American families: Risk factors and adaptations to violence in 8,145 families.* New Brunswick: Transaction Publishers.

Straus, M. A., Gelles, R. J., & Steinmetz, S. K. (1980). *Behind closed doors: A survey of family violence in America.* New York: Doubleday.

Tangney, J. P. (1991). Moral affect: The good, the bad, and the ugly. *Journal of Personality and Social Psychology, 61*, 598–607.

Tangney, J. P., Wagner, P., Fletcher, C., & Gramzow, R. (1992). Shamed into anger? The relation of shame and guilt to anger and self-reported aggression. *Journal of Personality and Social Psychology, 62*, 669–675.

Tannen, D. (1991). *You just don't understand: Women and men in conversation.* New York: William Morrow

Tavris, C. (1987). *Anger: The misunderstood emotion.* New York: Simon & Schuster

Tice, D. (1992, August). *Anger regulation strategies.* Paper presented to the annual meeting of the American Psychological Association, Washington, DC.

Tolman, R. M., & Bennett, L. W. (1990). A review of quantitative research on men who batter. *Journal of Interspersonal Violence, 5*, 87–118.

Tomkins, S. S. (1963). *Affect, imagery, consciousness, Vol II.* New York: Springer Publishing Co.

Tomkins, S. S. (1991). *Affect, imagery, consciousness, Vol IV.* New York: Springer Publishing Co.

Vaillant, G. E. (1977). Theoretical hierarchy of adaptive ego mechanisms: A 30–year follow-up of 30 men selected for psychological health. *Archives of General Psychiatry, 24*, 107–117.

van der Kolk, B. E. (1989). The compulsion to repeat the trauma: Re-enactment, revictimization, and masochism. *Psychiatric Clinics of North America, 12*(2), 388–411.

Van Hasselt, V. B., Morrison, R. L., & Bellock, A. S. (1985). Alcohol use in wife abusers and their spouses. *Addictive Behaviors, 10*, 127–135.

Waas, G. A. (1988). Social attributional biases of peer-rejected and aggressive children. *Child Development, 59*, 969–992.

Walker, L. (1980) *The battered woman.* New York: Harper & Row.

Walker, L. (1984). *The battered woman syndrome.* New York: Springer Publishing Co.

Walker, L. (1989a). *Terrifying love.* New York: Harper Perennial.

Weeks, J. (1984). *Aging: Concepts and social issues.* Belmont, CA: Wadsworth.

Weiss, R. S. (1982). Attachment in adult life. In C. M. Parkes & J. Stevenson-Hinde (Eds.), *The place of attachment in human behavior* (pp. 171–184). New York: Basic Books.

Weisfeld, G. (1994). Aggression and dominance in the social world of boys. In J. Archer (Ed.), *Male violence* (pp. 23–41). London: Routledge.

West, M. & Sheldon, A. (1988). Classification of pathological attachment patterns in adults. *Journal of Personality Disorders, 2,* 153–159.

West, M. L. & Sheldon-Keller, A. E. (1994). *Patterns of relating.* New York: Guilford Press.

White, G. L., & Mullen, P. E. (1989). *Jealousy: Theory, research, and clinical strategies.* New York: Guilford.

Whiteman, M., Fanshel, D., & Grundy, J. F. (1987). Cognitive-behavioral interventions aimed at anger of parents at risk of child abuse. *Social Work, 32,* 469–474.

Wiehe, V. R. (1987). Empathy and locus of control in child abusers. *Journal of Social Service Research, 9*(2/3), 17–30.

Williams, R. B., Haney, T. L., Lee, K. L., Kong, Y., Blumenthal, J., & Whalen, R. E. (1980). Type A behavior, hositilty, and coronary atherosclerosis. *Psychosomatic Medicine, 42* 539–549.

Williams, R. B., & Williams, V. (1993). *Anger kills.* New York: Times Books.

Wills, T. A. (1981). Downward comparison principles in social psychology. *Psychological Bulletin, 90,* 245–272.

Wolpe, J. (1958). *Psychotherapy by reciprocal inhibition.* Palo Alto, CA: Stanford University Press.

Wong, M. M., & Csikszentmihalyi, M. (1991). Affiliation motivation and daily experience: Some issues on gender differences. *Journal of Personality and Social Psychology, 60,* 154–164.

Young, G. H. (1990). *Spouse abuse and patterns of attachment.* Dissertations Abstracts International.

Zillmann, D. (1978). *Hostility and aggression.* Hillsdale, NJ: Erlbaum.

Appendix A

Pilot Evaluation of the Compassion Workshop

WHY FOCUS ON MALE SPOUSE ABUSERS?

Three rationales might persuade clinicians dedicated to the amelioration of attachment abuse to focus treatment efforts on male abusers of their female lovers. First, it is the type of attachment abuse most connected to the other forms, overlapping with both child and elder-parent abuse. Second, witnessing the abuse of their mother is clearly damaging to children (Kashani, Daniel, Dandoy, & Holcomb, 1992). Though not as yet empirically studied, it takes little clinical sensitivity to discern the damage to an elder-parent in witnessing the abuse of an adult daughter. Although it is possible to hide child abuse from a spouse and elder abuse from a spouse and children, spouse abuse seems much more difficult to conceal. It would seem that spouse abuse can affect the entire family in ways that child and elder-parent abuse may not. Finally, because male abusers are the adult group least proficient at the critical skills of attachment and affect regulation, and the most resistant to successful treatment, a treatment protocol that works for them should offer similar success with other forms of attachment abuse.

DESIGN

The design of the pilot study to evaluate the Compassion Workshop was pretest, posttest experimental, with standard agency treatment serving as comparison group.[1] Assignment to either treatment group was random. The 1-year follow-up measurement of the abuse variables was made exclusively from the report of victims.

SUBJECTS

Men entering treatment for spouse abuse in each of the five participating community mental health centers served as subjects for the study. Due to demographic differences among the populations of the various mental health centers, each center had its own randomly assigned treatment groups. All experimental and comparison groups were pooled for analysis. Of the 122 invited to participate in the experiment, 100 (82%) accepted.

The integrity of random assignment was tested with logistical regression analysis with group membership as the dependent variable. The only significant differences between groups were in level of violence and verbal aggression. But this was an expected artifact. The participation of spouses in

[1]Treatment at the five community mental health centers in Maryland and Virginia participating in the study consisted of five different variations of the prevailing group-interventions described in the literature of spouse abuse (e.g., Tolman & Bennett, 1990). All stressed cognitive-behavioral interventions, focusing on anger and stress management, assertiveness training, alternative strategies in conflict resolution, and altering attitudes toward women and relationships. Treatment tended toward the didactic and included videos, slides, handouts, homework, and client-kept anger logs. There were frequent and vigorous confrontations of any attitudes against women or for male entitlement. Partners were not included in the treatment and were never systematically contacted by group leaders during the course of treatment. Group sessions often began with check-ins, during which each client told about his week and the content of his anger log. Group leaders ranged from trained volunteers to experienced social workers and psychologists. Consistent with findings of psychotherapy in general, trained volunteers did as well as the professionals in these highly structured curricula.

Table A.1 Sample Size by Data Collection Point

Parameter	*Treatment subjects*	*Control subjects*
Recruited	50	50
Pretest responses	45	50
Treatment exit responses	38	24
1 year follow-up of abuse variables reported by female partners	31	32

the experimental group invoked the widely documented higher incidence of abuse reported by spouses. The artifact was controlled in outcome analyses by only considering report of spouses from both groups. With this adjustment, there were no pretest differences between the groups; both were in the 98 percentile of violence, according to the norms of the Conflict Tactics Scale (Straus, 1979) (See Tables A.1, A.2).

MEASURES

The Conflict Tactics Scale

The Conflict Tactics Scale (CTS) (Straus, 1979), the most frequently used instrument in domestic violence research, has been widely tested for validity and reliability (Allen & Straus, 1979; Claes & Rosenthal, 1990; Straus, 1973, 1974; Straus et al., 1980). A 19-item, 6-point, zero-anchored, Likert-type, self-report inventory, the CTS consists of a list of actions a spouse might take in a conflict with a partner. Scoring was weighted in the manner suggested by Straus and Gelles (1988), to yield a simultaneous measure of violence severity and frequency. Because weighting created an extremely skewed distribution, the variable was dichotomized for analysis. Incidents of violence equal to, or more severe than, two pushes, grabs, or shoves, were coded as 1. The cut-off for

Table A.2 Sample Characteristics

Parameters	*Treatment group*	*Control group*
n	45	50
Race		
Black	44%	45%
White	47%	45%
Hispanic	4%	5%
Asian	5%	5%
Mean education	12.61 years	12.41 years
Mean age	33 years	35 years
Median income	$25,000	$25,000
Referral source		
Court-ordered/pressured	84%	87%
Self-referral	16%	13%
Head injury		
Yes	24%	19%
No	76%	81%
Criminal charges for spouse abuse		
One	100%	100%
Two	51%	58%
Three or More	18%	18%
Self-report criminal history		
Assault Nondomestic	7%	8%
Other charges	40%	42%
Violence in family of origin		
Yes	52%	52%
No	48%	48%
Personal alcohol problem		
Yes	40%	53%
No	60%	47%

verbal aggression was 12, the norm for the scale in the general population.[2]

Because abusers tend to underreport their acts of aggression, the CTS was also administered by phone to the

[2]Even with the dichotomization of the violence variable, there remained some gain from weighting, enabling comparison in terms of frequency and severity of violence for the year before and the year after treatment.

spouse or significant other of each subject, with the abuser's behavior toward her as the reference point of the items. The higher of the two data sources was counted, in accordance with convention (Straus & Gelles, 1988). Follow-up measurement of abuse variables included only cases where subjects spent 2 or more days per week with their spouses/significant others, and only when report of the victim was available.

The Rosenberg Self-Esteem Scale

In the past 5 years, Rosenberg's (1965) concise scale has been used nearly five times more frequently (48 studies) in research than its nearest competitor instrument (Cribb, Ozone, & Pipes, 1992). The 10-item scale in the Likert format has demonstrated high internal consistency and good convergent validity with other measures of self-esteem (Demo, 1985).[3]

The Causal Dimension Scale

Abusers' acceptance of responsibility for their own behavior is discussed in virtually every treatment article as a necessary condition for ending abuse. The construct was measured by a modified version of the locus of causality subscale of the Likert-type Causal Dimension Scale (Russell, 1982). Internal consistency reliability of the locus of causality subscale is 0.88 (Russell, 1982). The modification for the current study asked respondents to "Think about the reason or reasons you typically engage in any instance of hitting, pushing, slapping, kicking, grabbing (or threats to do any of these to) your spouse or significant other. The items below concern your impressions or opinions of the cause or causes of the behavior."

[3]Due to a misprint in the instrument packet, only nine of the 10 items were scored. This adjustment had no affect on the internal consistency of the scale.

The Symptom Questionnaire

Anger–hostility, anxiety, and well-being are important concepts relative to the causal theory of attachment abuse presented in these pages. Changes in these variables at posttest indicate changes in the construction of meaning of subjects. The variables were measured by the pertinent subscales of the Symptom Questionnaire, a self-report, "yes or no" instrument in wide clinical and research use (Kellner, 1987). The anger-hostility and anxiety subscales are 17 items each, with six additional items to measure well-being embedded in each subscale. Results of reliability trials demonstrate that the subscales rate in the low .90s. Validity studies reported by Kellner (1987) establish criterion and construct validity for the instrument.

At pretest, the current sample scored moderately distressed on all three subscales, more than a standard deviation apart from published norms (Kellner, 1987).

Violence-Anger Regulation Strategies

Strategies to regulate affect and behavior have been linked empirically and theoretically to the successful regulation of affect and behavior (Baumeister, 1991; Rohde, Lewihsohn, Tilson, & Seele, 1990; Rosenbaum, 1980; Tice, 1992). Subjects were asked two questions, ("List the things you typically do to avoid *violence* against your spouse or significant other:" and, "List the things you typically do when you are *angry* or about to *become* angry at your spouse or significant other:"). Space was allowed for up to 10 strategies. Scoring consisted of coding the strategies into the following categories: 0 = confrontation, 1 = none, 2 = escape, 3 = resolution. In the data analysis, the variables were dichotomized, excluding the escape code: 0 = no resolution strategies, 1 = resolution strategies. Because nearly all respondents wrote the same thing for both questions, they were combined in analysis.

The Attachment Compassion Scale

The Attachment Compassion Scale is a 10-item, 5-point Likert-type, self-report instrument designed for the current study. Because no precedents for measuring compassion could be found, the construct, for measurement purposes, was considered equivalent to the construct of empathy. Involving cognitive, affective, and communicative dimensions (Harman, 1986), empathy is defined as "the intellectual or imaginative apprehension of another's condition or state of mind without actually experiencing that person's feelings" (Hogan, 1969, p. 307).[4] Of course, the experience of empathy or compassion depends on being able to apprehend another's condition or state of mind, that is, to take another's perspective. Existing empathy scales were eschewed for the proposed study due to their global qualities and their inappropriateness for use in spouse abuse research. The perspective-taking inherent in the sort of empathy–compassion apposite to attachment abuse need not extend beyond familial ties and must take place under the fire of emotional conflict.

The Attachment Compassion Scale was constructed to measure:

1. self-perceived ability to employ perspective-taking when angry;
2. well-being provided by the experience of compassion;
3. motivation to do good for one's attachment figure.

Internal consistency reliability, checked with the data set from the study (n = 100), resulted in an alpha of 0.86. A meager argument for criterion validity is based on correlations with instruments measuring similar constructs, shown in previous research to be valid. The Spouse Compassion Scale correlated with the Rosenberg Self-Esteem Scale = .66, $p < .01$, two-tailed, and the well-being subscale of the Symp-

[4]Compassion differs from empathy in that the former includes both motivation to act and self-enhancement, as well as understanding of, and sympathy with, others.

tom Questionnaire = .49, $p < .01$, two-tailed. Spearman's Rho was used to test associations with the nonlinear variables of the anger–hostility subscale of the Symptom Questionnaire = −.29, $p < .05$, two-tailed and the anxiety subscale = −.24, $p < .05$, two-tailed. In addition, the compassion scale correlated with strategies to resolve anger and violence .39, $p < .05$, two-tailed.

Evidence of construct validity, indicating an inverse relationship between compassion and abuse, centers on the Spearman's Rho correlation of −.23 ($p < .05$, two-tailed) with weighted violence score of the CTS and −.19 ($p < .05$, two-tailed) with the verbal aggression scores.

"*Belief that domestic violence is a serious social problem*" is an important component of the standard agency treatment. On a 5-point Likert scale, subjects were asked whether the following statement accurately described their opinions: "I think violence between husbands and wives (or men and their girlfriends) is overrated as a social problem."

The CAGE Questionnaire for Alcohol Abuse

The CAGE questionnaire (Ewing & Rouse, 1970) is a 4-item instrument for the detection of alcohol abuse. The items are scored in yes or no categories. Widely used in social science and medical research, the CAGE has been judged to be a particularly sensitive, reliable, and valid instrument for the detection of alcohol problems (Bush, Shaw, Cleary, Delbanco, & Aronson, 1987; Ewing, 1984; Mayfield, McLeod, & Hall, 1974).

PROCEDURE

In all cases, pretests were given to subjects before they were aware of group assignment. Spouses/significant others were given the CTS by phone, administered by research assistants. *The spouses were asked to keep track of any verbal or physical aggression that occurred in the future.* Posttests were given immediately following treatment for the experimental group and after the 13th week of the comparison groups. The comparison groups met for 24 weeks, except for two of the groups, which met for 18 weeks. It was decided to give the posttests in the middle of treatment for the comparison groups to maintain consistency of time between pre- and posttests. The rationale is the inherent unfairness in giving the comparison groups 6 to 12 more weeks to re-abuse.

Measuring the other variables in the middle of the comparison treatment invites the argument that the comparison treatment did not have time to affect well-being, anxiety, anger, hostility, etc. However, this point pales next to the overriding purpose of the treatment: to stop abuse quickly and completely. Change in the well-being, distress, and beliefs of abusers are important only insofar as they contribute to the relief of victims. Even if the comparison treatments catch-up to the Compassion Workshop by the end of their longer duration, that would be an important occurrence only if it parallels a downward movement in the abuse variables, which were measured 1 year following completion of the treatment. A third possibility—measuring the abuse variables at equal time durations for both groups, while measuring the other variables at the completion of both groups—was eschewed for the following reason. It was feared that contact with the spouses for posttest data a full 6 to 12 weeks before the men in the comparison group were contacted, could agitate the paranoid jealousy exhibited by so many in this treatment population (see Chapter 3).

RESULTS

The dependent variables were the only significant differences between the groups at posttest (See Table A.3). In other words, differential attrition did not destroy the effects of random assignment.

Table A.3 Outcome Variables

Variable	Compassion Workshop	Comparison
Violence free		
1 year after treatment		
n	31	32
%	87% (27)[d]	41% (13)[d]
Verbal aggression free		
1 year after treatment		
n	31	32
%	71% (22)[c]	25% (8)[c]
Reduced violence		
1 year after treatment		
n	31	32
%	97%[b]	53%[b]
Reduced verbal aggression		
1 year after treatment		
n	31	32
%	65%[b]	35%[b]
Self-responsibility for abuse		
n	33	20
Rate of improvement from pretest	31%[c]	0
Self-responsibility for anger		
n	34	20
Rate of improvement from pretest	65%[c]	0
Perceives domestic violence as important social problem		
n	34	20
Rate of improvement from pretest	65%[c]	−4%[NS]
Strategies to resolve anger and avoid violence		
n	37	32
Rate of improvement from pretest	95%[c]	77%[c]
Compassion for spouse		
n	33	20
Rate improvement from pretest	37%[c]	4%[NS]
Well-being		
n	34	23
Rate of improvement from pretest	30%[c]	9%[NS]
Self-esteem		
n	35	21
Rate of improvement from pretest	8%[b]	1%[NS]

Variable	*Compassion Workshop*	*Comparison*
Anger-hostility		
n	34	23
Rate of improvement from pretest	63%[c]	48%[a]
Anxiety		
n	34	23
Rate of improvement from pretest	60%[c]	26%[NS]
attendance		
10–12 sessions	69% (31)[b]	28% (14)[b]
6–9 sessions	91% (41)[b]	62% (31)[b]

[a] < .05; [b] < .01; [c] < .001.
[NS] No statistical significance.

Although not directly related to hypothesis testing, a somewhat surprising finding is the relationship of number of times spanked during childhood to the pretest dependent variables and to a number of negative variables (See Table A.4).

Table A.4 Correlations of Times Spanked in Childhood with Pretest, Variable

anger-hostility	= .24[a]
anxiety	= .35[b]
Cage score	= .25[a]
disorderly conduct arrests	= .24[a]
family problems	= .38[b]
head injury	= .28[b]
education	= −.31[b]
self-esteem	= −.36[b]
violence in childhood	= .47[b]
verbal aggression	= .51 (Spearman's Rho)[b]
violence against spouse	= .24 (Spearman's Rho)[a]
racial minorities	= .35[b]
not court-ordered	= .32[b]

[a] = $p < .05$, two-tailed
[b] = $p < .01$, two-tailed

DISCUSSION

In this preliminary study, the Compassion Workshop greatly reduced violence, verbal aggression, anger–hostility, and anxiety, while significantly improving well-being, strategies to avoid anger-violence, acceptance of personal responsibility, and belief that domestic violence is a serious social problem. Collectively these data offer at least some support for the contention that the men underwent changes in constructions of meaning that greatly reduced their tendencies toward abuse.

Both groups considerably reduced anger, a pretreatment correlate of physical and verbal aggression. The observed posttreatment differences in violence and verbal aggression suggest that the *way* anger was reduced may be a key factor in preventing abuse. These results support the findings that taking another's perspective causes an emotional response that is incompatible with anger, hostility, and aggression against that person (e.g., Baron, 1984). The experience of compassion seems to have a simultaneous healing effect on the hurt for which the anger and hostility were a defense; it increased well-being and made it increasingly more rewarding to take the perspective of another. It would seem that to understand deeply the hurt of another is to heal one's own hurt, possibly because the act of deep, cognitive-affective understanding integrates diverse aspects of the self and makes us feel uniquely whole.

Attitudes

The finding of increased belief in the Compassion Workshop subjects that domestic violence is a serious social problem came about, as hypothesized, even though the treatment made no mention of domestic violence as a social problem. In contrast, the standard agency treatment made the social context of spouse abuse a major component of its protocol, yet failed to produce a significant change on this variable, even from within-group pretest scores. (In fact, there was a nonsignificant 4% *reduction* in the belief that spouse abuse was a serious social problem among comparison group subjects.) This finding lends support to the constructivist view that attitudes are mere reflections of constructions of meaning. Treatments based on changing reflections rather than causes run a high risk of getting lost in a hall of mirrors.

Locus of Causality

The movement toward internal locus of causality in Compassion Workshop subjects is especially promising. As long as responsibility is kept distinct from blame, clients will find reward in acceptance of responsibility. A basic tenet of the treatment is that blame is the activity of victims, who condemn themselves to chronic feelings of powerlessness, whereas responsibility paves the realm of the personally powerful.

Dropouts

The differential early dropout rate in favor of the Compassion Workshop group confirms the results of an experiment testing the video, *Shadows of the Heart,* as an effective instrument for immediately engaging spouse abusers in treatment (Stosny, 1994).

Pretreatment Findings

Data concerning the pretreatment sample confirm what is generally known about spouse abusers (e.g., Tolman & Bennett, 1990): low levels of self-esteem and well-being, high levels of anger, hostility, and anxiety, external locus of control, and external attributions of causality for abusive behavior.

The Ills of Spanking Children

The significant correlation of times-spanked with pretreatment dependent variables of distress, low self-esteem, violence, and verbal aggression is surprising in this violent population, especially with a relatively low response ceiling. (The highest category was spanked "more than 30 times" in 18 years). One might expect that common childhood spanking would have little effect in the presence of so many other problems. That the associations with the dependent variables vanished in the Compassion Workshop group after treatment suggests that the negative effects of spanking children are, at least, remediable.

LIMITATIONS OF THE STUDY

A major limitation of the study is one of construct validity, in that it offers no control for therapist effects. Although no clinician should bring anything less than fervor and commitment to whatever treatment of clients he employs, the developer of a treatment must have a more intense commitment to the treatment he delivers than someone who adopts a protocol developed by others. This problem was only exacerbated in the current study by the developer of the treatment serving as its evaluator. His commitment to the treatment could inadvertently affect his recording and interpretation of the data. For these reasons, the current study can serve as no more than a pilot for a larger-scale effort that randomly assigns therapists and clients to treatment conditions.

It is difficult to assess the effects of resentful demoralization on the internal validity of this study of a resistant treatment population. One can only speculate about the effect of assignment to a comparison group, rather than a treatment group designed to boost self-esteem, pride, and compassion, on men lacking all of these, but who feel angry and humiliated about being forced into treatment in the first place. It does not appear that resentful demoralization had an effect on the dropout rate, which was equivalent to the norm for the participating agencies in working with this population. It's important to note that no one who dropped out of the study remained in treatment. In other words, they were dissuaded from the standard agency treatment itself, which failed to engage clients, most of whom were court-ordered to submit to it. On the other hand, resentful demoralization may account for the relatively low rate of comparison group spouses completing the CTS. Whatever the effects of resentful demoralization, they could have been mitigated only slightly by the offer of free exposure to the Compassion Workshop after the posttest, an offer of which no one took advantage.

FUTURE RESEARCH

Studies that seek to document change in emotional abuse should use measures that are sensitive to belated breaks in habitual verbal patterns.[5] Immediately apologizing for an insult or spiteful remark cannot be equivalent, in terms of coercion or emotional damage, to a willful, mean-spirited verbal assault. Thus qualitative and level of intensity measures are needed.

Structured Victim Logs

Researchers should consider providing victims with logs to keep track of incidents of verbal and physical aggression during periods of study. In the current work, the women were merely asked at initial contact to keep track of abusive incidents for the posttest and follow-up calls, but were not instructed to do so. At posttest, some women who kept written logs on their own, reported that the record keeping helped them recall incidents of minor violence as well as verbal aggression.

Ethical Demands

An ethical imperative for those who treat abusers is to carefully and continuously evaluate the effectiveness of clinical

[5]Unfortunately, the CTS provides no measure of apology for or withdrawal of the insult. Frequently women in the current study reported that their spouses would start into a cursing tirade, remember their new anger-regulation techniques, stop themselves, and then apologize to resolve the conflict. This is not reflected in the CTS score, which merely counts incidents of insults.

intervention. A deeply painful part of the current study came in phoning comparison-group women who were continuing to be abused while staying with their abusers through a treatment they desperately hoped would be effective. Unfortunately, provider agencies—mostly private, nonprofits with little oversight or funds to employ professional clinicians—seem to regard evaluation of their abuser programs as an anathema. Only one agency in the entire, statewide Maryland Network against Domestic Violence and a similar organization in Northern Virginia, reported outcome data of any kind of methodologically sound evaluation (with findings nearly identical to the standard agency treatment results reported in the current work). A similar lack of program evaluation has been reported by other researchers (e.g., Dankwort, 1991). This may be due to the fact that many clinicians who treat abusers realize the impotence of the treatment (Dankwort, 1991). The authors of the most popular "treatment" model for spouse abusers, Pence and Paymar (1993), "have no illusion that most men will stop their violence and give up their power" (p. xiv). I have yet to meet a clinician who honestly feels his treatment is effective with abusers. Most argue that reducing violence even a little (even when increasing emotional abuse) is worth the effort. But with this volatile treatment population, lack of practice evaluation crosses the line separating merely bad practice from the unethical, because many victims remain with their abusers in the too often illusory hope of treatment effectiveness. I know that the Compassion Workshop will prove effective on at least seven of 10 abusers, yet I would not want it used without continual standardized evaluation.

PTSD and Anger

More systematic research into the nature of the Post-traumatic Stress Disorder (PTSD) symptoms exhibited by victims in this project is urgently needed. The urgency comes not only from the observations of other researchers concerning these symptoms in victims of spouse abuse (e.g., Janoff-Bulman, & Frieze, 1983; Walker, 1984), but from recent suggestive findings about the relationship of anger to PTSD symptoms. Although elevated anger has long been associated with PTSD (Riggs et al., 1992), Riggs and his colleagues provide the first longitudinal connection, which suggests that the level of anger predicts the onset and severity of PTSD symptoms. Some 116 women who had been recent victims of sexual and nonsexual criminal assault were assessed for levels of anger and hostility within a month of their assault. One month later—the minimum required time for the diagnosis of PTSD—86 of the women were located for reassessment. Analysis indicated a significant predictive function of earlier anger scores to both the occurrence and severity of PTSD symptoms.

The importance of these findings to attachment abuse lies in the use of anger as a mobilizing force in the profeminist treatment of victims (Walker, 1984). Such treatment may unwittingly exacerbate, if not create, PTSD symptoms in a cruel and ironic kind of re-victimization. As discussed in Chapter 3, although anger is a potent mobilizer, it greatly impairs cognitive functioning, especially judgment. The mobilization of anger comes at a dangerously high price for PTSD sufferers, already scarred by the teeth of depression, as the amphetamine-like rush of the anger–arousal cycle resolves once again in depression, probably through depletion of norepinephrine. It is not difficult to stimulate anger in persons who are hurt. But competent and sensitive treatment requires healing the hurt, rather than using it as the churning fuel for anger that will not be stilled until the hurt is regulated. That anger is an effective *motivator* goes without question. That it is a dangerous and damaging *regulator* for vulnerable subjects should be apparent, as Walker cautions elsewhere in *The Battered Woman Syndrome* (1984).

The *HEALS* technique proved highly effective in helping victims regulate the hurt that stimulated their anger. As a result, they felt more in control of their internal experience. This allowed many of them to make rational decisions about whether to repair the damaged attachment bonds with their former abusers or to end the relationships. In either case, they were free to pursue a course of self-actualization so long denied them by the alternating terror, residual anger, and depression caused by abuse at the hands of those they love.

Measuring Attitudes

In replications of this study, broader measures of attitudes toward women, patriarchy, and the larger social context of domestic violence should be employed, with the hypothesis that the Compassion Workshop, which does not include these elements, will produce higher levels of attitudes favorable to the profeminist approach than will profeminist treatments. This will constitute evidence that negative attitudes, like those that seem to justify the exertion of power and control over women, are mere symptoms of the necessary condition for abuse, that is, the abuser's experience of an internal power void. Once men are given the remedial skill to fill the internal power-voids that ruin their lives and the lives of their loved ones, the subjugation and abuse of women will be relegated to a nightmare of the brutal past.

Note: Since the study ended, the Compassion Workshop has been established in Prince George's County, Maryland, with the special help of the Honorable Theresa Nolan, Judge of the District Court and Chair of the Domestic Violence Coordinating Committee. As of June 1995, more than 300 participants have been treated. At 1 year follow-up with the CTS, 89% of victims report that they are violence-free, and 81% report that they are free of verbal aggression.

Appendix B

The Attachment Compassion Scale

Please answer the following questions with the number that most accurately describes your impressions.

5 Strongly agree
4 Agree
3 Unsure
2 Disagree
1 Strongly disagree

When I am very angry at my wife (or significant other), and I think about her point of view or how she is feeling:

a. I feel angrier. ____
b. I feel kinder toward her. ____
c. I feel warmer toward her. ____
d. I feel furious. ____
e. I don't care about her point of view, at least not until I cool down. ____
f. I feel more patient. ____
g. I feel like I should give her support and sympathy. ____
h. I feel like I should apologize for hurting her feelings. ____
i. I feel charitable, forgiving. ____
j. I find that I can't think about what she's feeling, until I cool down. ____

Index

U

V

W